To Dear Mark
Hope you eyo,

Love Aunty Helen & David
September 2010

BAKING for BLOKES

This book is for my brother, Bones. Not many of us could work 200 feet (60 m) in the air, wearing a boiler suit, balancing on a thin steel pole whilst welding seams into explosive materials at temperatures of up to 3000°C.

Bones does that and more on a daily basis. At least, I think that's what he does.

He's a heck of a Bloke. Shame he can't bake (yet).

BAKING
for BLOKES
DIY in the Kiwi kitchen

STEVE JOLL

First published in 2010 by New Holland Publishers (NZ) Ltd
Auckland • Sydney • London • Cape Town

www.newhollandpublishers.co.nz

218 Lake Road, Northcote, Auckland 0627, New Zealand
Unit 1, 66 Gibbes Street, Chatswood, NSW 2067, Australia
86–88 Edgware Road, London W2 2EA, United Kingdom
80 McKenzie Street, Cape Town 8001, South Africa

Copyright © 2010 in text: Steve Joll
Copyright © 2010 in illustrations: Steve Joll
Copyright © 2010 New Holland Publishers (NZ) Ltd

Publishing manager: Christine Thomson
Editor: Renée Lang
Design: Grace Design

National Library of New Zealand Cataloguing-in-Publication Data

Joll, Steve.
Baking for blokes : DIY in the kiwi kitchen / Steve Joll.
Includes index.
ISBN 978-1-86966-293-6
1. Cookery. I. Title.
641.512—dc 22

10 9 8 7 6 5 4 3 2 1

Colour reproduction by Image Centre Ltd., Auckland
Printed by Tien Wah Press (Pte) Ltd

Contents

How it all began

THERE I WAS AT THE DAIRY buying a bunch of stuff I'd run out of (butter, flour, eggs) and when I plonked the whole lot down on the counter the woman smiled at me and said, 'Is your wife doing some baking this afternoon, then?'

'No,' I told her with a friendly smile. 'I am.' Her reaction was a raised, all-knowing eyebrow. I might as well have said I was off home to put on stockings and a pink nightie and dance around the lounge to the *Village People's Greatest Hits* waving a feather boa and pouting my pretty red lips.

To be fair, she's not the only person to have raised an eyebrow in the same way. Once, while chatting with Lenny Henry (who, by the way, is quite the little name dropper – unlike me, of course), I figured I'd found a kindred spirit – what with Lenny having played the role of Chef in the TV series of the same name. I told him about my love of baking. And he laughed. Out loud. In an 'at-you-not-with-you' kind of way.

It seems in this modern, enlightened age you can paint rainbows, cut your hair like David Beckham, quaff wine and plant a veggie garden – but baking is still seen as a woman's domain.

Well, not any more, my friends. Baking is just like DIY: it's precise and takes a steady hand, it's about building and sharing the results of your labour, it means following a strict set of instructions and yet it's also about being creative. And for blokes the best thing about baking is this: you get to eat the results.

On the back of the abuse, the funny looks and the raised eyebrows I decided to kick off a website for blokes who bake. It turns out there are a few of us and from the website this book was born.

Who this book is for

ONE OF THE MOST common questions I get asked via my website is: 'I'm not a bloke, can I still use the recipes?'

Of course you can! Assuming you can handle the jandal. By which I mean, if you're okay with things being written in a fairly straightforward way without lots of floury (excuse the pun) language and assumptions.

I don't know about you, but I get sick of trying recipes that call for all sorts of crazy ingredients that you have to source from specialist shops in the Big Smoke. And it's all very well for the people – mostly chefs (some of who are top blokes, by the way) – who write these books to say that baking is easy. Of course it's easy for them! They can julienne a carrot in 3.6 seconds. That's like Dan Carter telling you that kicking goals is a piece of, well, cake.

Baking for Blokes is full of simple recipes using ingredients you probably already have in the pantry and fridge. Most of the recipes can be made quickly – and even the ones that require a bit of messing around can be done in stages, or the day before, or whenever you have time.

The point of it is this: if I can do it, so can you. I'm an amateur baker who's taken the time to experiment and find what works and what doesn't and then written down the results. So if I tell you it's easy, then it really is.

This book is for Blokes and the Blokettes who love them. It's for good, sports-watching ladies and their lady-watching good sorts. Men, women, old or young, if you enjoy whipping out your muffins at the most appropriate moment – enjoy.

Things you should know before you start

Credit where credit's due

The recipes in this book come from many sources. Some are old family favourites, some have come through my website (blokeswhobake.co.nz) and some have been given to me by friends. In every case, if I'm taking the credit then it's a recipe I've legitimately stolen, then altered and experimented with so I can call it my own.

In some cases I've loved a recipe 'as is'. There are some things you just don't mess with. Where that's happened, I've credited the genius behind the recipe.

Raise it yourself

I'm not the kind of bloke who keeps 10 different kinds of flour in the cupboard. So for the most part (with a couple of exceptions) I have stuck with a combination of standard flour and baking powder rather than the self-raising stuff. What you want to do is up to you.

Use your noodle

I've usually kept recipes separate and then, when it's appropriate, provided some options for good combinations. For example, instead of showing you how to make crêpes filled with chocolate mousse, I prefer to tell you how to make both of those elements. Then, if you want to stick them together, that's great. And if you want to use your crêpes another way, that's great too.

At the weigh-in

There's a lot of debate about whether folk these days prefer to measure in cups and tablespoons or grams and millilitres. I think it depends entirely upon what you're weighing. But for the sake of consistency in this book all flour and sugar, baking powder and so on (i.e. dry ingredients) is measured in cups or spoons – unless the amount is so small that it becomes fiddly, or not easily converted (e.g. 50 g flour equals 2/5ths of a cup or somewhere between 2–3 tablespoons, so 50 g is easier for all concerned). Butter is also measured in grams.

It's important to note here that a standard cup measure is 250 ml (1 cup of flour is 125 g). Make sure you have a standard measuring jug in your tool kit (see page 11).

Tin tin

It should be noted that I don't own and have never used the silicone baking or muffin trays. The preparation discussed in Top tips (see below) is for standard tin tins or spring-form tins.

The 'DOD' system

Each recipe in this book is rated somewhere between 1–5 based on ease and speed of preparation. Keep in mind that I don't think anything in this book is what you'd call very difficult, but at the less tricky end of the spectrum there's still a range. So if you want something super-quick and easy, look for the number 1 alongside the heading. For stuff that's a little more fiddly, or at the very least more time-consuming, it's probably going to be a number 4 or 5. But for the record, here's how my 'degree of difficulty' system works:

1. Very quick/Easy
2. Quick/Easy
3. Pretty quick/Pretty easy
4. Pretty lengthy/Pretty tricky
5. Lengthy/Very tricky

The tool kit

THERE ARE SOME THINGS you'll need and some things you'll want to have just to keep up with the Jones's. There are also a few items that ladies often use, but us blokes generally don't have to worry about because of our superior size and strength.

The 'MUST HAVES' in your tool kit

BBT (bloke's baking towel): the ultimate baking accessory, you can use this to wrap, grab, wipe, cover and flick. Also known as a tea towel, have it hanging over your left shoulder at all times when you're in the kitchen. Get one online at *Blokes Who Bake*. Yes, this *is* a shameless plug.

Spatula: sounds like a gladiator, doesn't it? (The kind to rise from the slave-pits to take on the evil emperor; 'I, Spatula' and all that). However, it's a tool handy for folding and scooping and spreading and licking.

Sharp knife: the sharper the better. Get a whole chopping block full with different sizes – and don't let your wife use them. Tell her in no uncertain terms that they're *your* baking knives whenever she tries it on.

Whisk: it's handy to have a couple in different sizes. Note that spending a little more and getting a good one will save your forearms a lot of pain.

Muffin trays: there's no manly way to say 'muffin tray', but prepare yourself to own at least two of them: a six-tray (man-sized muffins to feed the boys) and a mini-muffin tray (fun for the kids). Those 12-tray jobs are all very well, but they seem a little undecided for my liking . . . trying to have a bob each way.

Cake tin: one that measures 20 cm across is pretty standard. And life will be a lot easier for you if it's spring-form. That is, if it has a removable base and sides that clip out.

Chopping board: wooden, please. Preferably one that you've made yourself from the base of a tree that you had to cut down with your own

chainsaw. Just kidding. I like the wooden ones is all.

Measuring jug: buy one of those tempered glass jugs that's marked with different measures so you can see how much 250 ml actually is. A fairly big one that will fit 2 full cups of flour saves mucking around. In fact, I reckon it saves a lot of hassle to have two of them.

Bowls: you just need a couple of these – good and big so you can get your mitts in there from time to time – and one of them should be metal so you can set up a bain marie (more about this later).

Hand-held electric beater: this is your Number One power tool (don't even think of substituting a drill attachment!).

The 'SHOULD HAVES' in your tool kit

Wooden spoon: your normal metal spoon will do the job, but a wooden one is good to have just because it's bigger. Man-sized fists don't wrap properly around standard spoons when they've got to stir heavy dough.

Rolling pin: if you don't have one, you can use a wine bottle or grab a full-sized beverage from the crate.

Measuring spoons: useful for measuring out very small quantities (e.g. ¼ teaspoon). Let's face it, they're not essential but those sets where each spoon fits inside the other can be handy. And if you need to be very specific, with measuring spoons you'll at least get the quantity right.

Sieve: as we mention in Top tips a fork will do the job, but a sieve is preferable and will save you fishing out lumps later on as well as helping to lighten the load by aerating the flour.

Scales: you really need these things for some recipes (unless, of course, you can figure out what constitutes 40 g of flour by holding it in your hand).

The 'I'm a show-off so I've got one. . .'

Melon baller: you'll be surprised how often this gadget comes in handy; making chocolate truffles is suddenly a lot easier.

Corer: makes putting together an apple or pear tart a lot faster.

Electric mixer with bowl and hook attachments: what a superb (but pricey) appliance – it'll keep your hands free so you can use the remote to flick between rugby and cricket or maybe swig on a little light refreshment.

Top tips

PLEASE FORGIVE ME if I'm telling you how to suck eggs here. You probably already know most of this stuff, but for those who want a little help – or find that things just ain't working out the way they should – the following tips might be of assistance.

Prep

Like any DIY project, the real success of your baking will lie in the preparation. Make sure you always:

- **Preheat the oven.**
- **Follow the instructions.** This includes putting ingredients into the mix in the right order. Baking is a bit like chemistry; you often need a reaction to take place between two ingredients which won't happen if you don't combine them in the right way.
- **Understand the lingo.** For example, softened butter is not the same as melted butter. There's more about this on page 14.
- **Grease or line the tin or tray** with baking paper and leave plenty of overhang so you can just lift the finished product out of the tin when it's done. If you're out of baking paper to line a tray, try using tinfoil. In fact I find it works really well when making a circular cake because it peels off so easily. Line the tin, grease the foil with butter and you'll be away laughing. I like to use butter for greasing, but spray oil will definitely save you time. Sometimes the recipe will tell you to dust a greased cake tin with flour or sugar, in which case make sure you do it – I can't stress this enough. I've had too many cakes fall apart because I haven't greased the tin or dusted it with flour.

Patience is often the key to getting the mixing right. A great example is squeezing butter through flour to make dough – take your time and do it right. The same applies to whisking and mixing. Do it thoroughly and you'll avoid lumps and bumps. Speaking of which, if you don't have a sieve or if it's already wet, put dry ingredients together and give them a good stir with a fork. A sieve gets rid of lumps in the flour and aerates it at the same time, but a fork can do almost the same thing.

Perfect pastry

There are a few little things you can do to make sure your shortcrust pastry comes out right every time. The first thing is to make sure the butter you use is good and cold. Chop it into small chunks or grate it and squeeze it through the flour really well. As mentioned already, patience is important here. Also, once it's made, don't over handle it, or you'll warm the butter too much. Press it with the heel of your hand into a disk shape and put the pastry back in the fridge for at least 30 minutes.

Creaming it

There's a big difference between creaming softened butter and melting it. The pros will use a bain marie to soften butter. That is, they get some water to a low boil in a pot, then put the butter in a metal bowl which goes into the hot water. The butter will start to melt, tip in your sugar and whisk. That's the right way to soften butter. Some blokes I know just zap it on low in the microwave. The main thing is, if you get the butter too hot it'll cook it and change the taste and texture.

When is enough enough?

When making muffins, fill the cups in the trays three-quarters full of mixture – any more and the results won't be pretty.

The right stuff

All ingredients are not born equal. Sometimes using a budget brand doesn't matter, sometimes it does. Generally speaking, butter and sugar is the same no matter whose name is on the wrapper. But it's important to get the good stuff when buying:

- **Flour:** quality is key and this is a key ingredient.
- **Cocoa:** I won't usually be this specific but the best I've found is Nestlé cocoa powder.
- **Chocolate:** brand doesn't matter but most cooking and baking chocolates are not made with cocoa butter. For best results you need at least 60 per cent cocoa butter where dark chocolate is called for.
- **Spices:** things like ginger, cinnamon and nutmeg are better bought at a specialty spice shop if you have one in town.
- **Vanilla:** while I've specified essence in most of the recipes in this book, I swear the results are a hundred times better if you chuck a vanilla pod into the liquid or use vanilla extract. Yes, it's pricey – but you can use the pods again and the taste is just so good.

OK, I think that's all the formalities out of the way. Now, I want a good clean fight, no punching below the belt, may the best bloke win and – at the bell – come out baking. Ding, ding.

Biscuits, Squares *and* Slices

Understanding the Lingo

Folding. (v) pron: PHOL-din'

a) *Accepting that your pair of threes is not going to beat whatever the other guy has.*
b) *Helping the Missus put away large laundry items such as sheets.*
c) *Making a paper crane or plane using the ancient art of Origami.*

YOU'LL SEE FOLDING mentioned a lot in recipe books. It's often used when you're mixing wet and dry ingredients or heavy ingredients with lighter ones.

Here's a tip: The way most people fold is to go around the outside with the spoon or spatula and then fold over into the middle. It works better by going the other way; down through the middle pulling the flat part of the spatula toward you and then up around the outside. You can do whatever you like but when it says 'fold' it means 'don't mix furiously'. Be gentle.

'It's hip to be square'
– *Huey Lewis and the News*

'Me want cookie!'
– *Cookie Monster*

FUDGE CAKE

IF I'M ALLOWED to say I have a signature dish, this is it. It's the first recipe I really mastered and just about the most commonly made thing in our excuse for a kitchen.

My dad and step-mum used to send food parcels down from Wanganui when I was a poor, starving single. You know the kind of thing – coffee, jams, a six-pack of amber ale and, best of all, homemade fudge. I couldn't rip that box open fast enough and my friends came to love the biscuity, chocolatey fudge so much I had to get the recipe and start making the stuff myself.

And the best part is that it's the most fun thing to make, probably because being too physical can be seen as politically incorrect – unless you're on a rugby field. So here's a chance to let loose, release some of that pent-up tension, holler a whole lot of abuse and generally work up a sweat (though if you're really going to go overboard on this I'd wait until no one else is home).

 THE KEY: Melt the sugar completely so you don't end up with a grainy texture.

TOP TIPS

Line the tin with baking paper so you can just lift out the cake when it's cooled.

You can mess around with whatever biscuits you prefer, but make sure they are not too thin (Wheatmeal or Digestives, for example, are worth a crack).

Degree of Difficulty: 2   **Makes** 30 squares

Ingredients

1 each packet of superwine and malt biscuits
150 g butter
1½ cups sugar
2 heaped tablespoons cocoa
2 eggs
chocolate icing, see page 161

Method

1. Wrap the biscuits in a tea towel and bash the living daylights out of them with a rolling pin. Brilliant! Now tip the bits into a large mixing bowl.
2. Chuck the butter and sugar into a decent-sized pot over a low heat – really low – and let it melt. Then tip in the cocoa and stir it through.
3. Throw the biscuit bits into the pot and mix them through. This will take a few minutes but it's important to make sure it's really well mixed. About now you're likely to be thinking you used too many biscuits – don't panic. It's supposed to be like that.
4. In a separate bowl beat the eggs until they're frothy. Tip them into the biscuit mix and stir through. Again, really work it around for a while, then pour the whole lot into a Swiss roll tin.
5. Make some chocolate icing (see page 161) and slather it over the top. Chuck the tin in the fridge and wait for about 1 hour before getting stuck in.

BLONDINI CAKE

THIS RECIPE is so blokey it once beat Ed Hillary to the top of a hill. It is so seriously manly they refused to allow it into the All Blacks on the grounds that the other jokers would feel inferior. This recipe is the kind of masculine that the SAS aspire to. There are tribes deep in the Amazon that regard this recipe as a deity.

The first time I baked this cake at home the wife thought I'd failed. Her exact words on sighting it were, 'Well, that didn't work.' Then she tasted it and her eyes danced a little, her mouth turned upward at each corner and she started to glow. That's how exceptional this recipe is – it got her pregnant! It ain't pretty – but there's a meal in every mouthful. Try it if you dare.

 THE KEY: Get the chocolate and butter mixed well at the start; otherwise the chocolate will sink to the bottom as the cake is baking.

Suggestions

- *Because the end product is pretty filling I cut it up into smallish fingers or squares, dust it with icing sugar and serve it with a little cream.*
- *For a change you could cut back to half a cup of rolled oats and put in half a cup of raisins or currants.*

Degree of Difficulty: 3   **Makes** about 35 squares

Ingredients

125 g butter, chopped

150 g white chocolate, chopped

¼ cup golden syrup

1 teaspoon vanilla essence

3 eggs

1 cup brown sugar, well packed

1½ cups standard flour

¼ teaspoon baking powder

⅔ cup rolled oats

½ cup shredded coconut

Oven temp:
160°C

Method

1. Preheat the oven to 160°C.
2. Line a large tin or baking dish (34 x 24 cm approx) with greased baking paper.
3. Melt the butter and chocolate together over a low heat.
4. Add the golden syrup and vanilla and whisk the whole lot until it's smooth.
5. In a separate bowl, whisk together the eggs and brown sugar until they're smooth and creamy. Then tip the butter/chocolate into the egg mixture and mix.
6. Add the rest of the ingredients (sifting the flour) and stir it all through with your trusty spatula until it's well sorted.
7. Tip the mixture into the baking dish and throw it in the oven.
8. Bake for about 50–60 minutes.

CHEWY CHOCOLATE CHIP COOKIES

THESE ARE SO GOOD it almost feels wrong. Forget that – it *is* wrong. But it's also so, so right. Big and chewy and gooey and delicious.

Remember being a wee lad pretending to be Hadlee in the back yard with your brother or father or sporty sister? For me, it was a time when the folks in the street all knew each other and no one had ever heard of the paparazzi. Think back to being a wee lad in those times as I try and put this recipe into context. If your standard chocolate chip biscuits are, say, the nice lady across the street who occasionally pops in to see your Mum, then these ones are her hot friend that you had a crush on.

THE KEY: Timing is everything. Get them out of the oven just as they start to colour up on top. They might seem to be a bit too soft, but once they cool you'll have the perfect biscuit.

TOP TIP

I find it easier to spoon the dough onto the baking tray if it's cooled a little first, so instead of the usual routine of preheating the oven while you mix the dough, do it the other way around. Mix the dough, then turn on the oven and while it's heating stick your mix in the fridge. It only needs a few minutes.

Degree of Difficulty: 2   **Makes** 14–16

Ingredients

180 g butter

1 cup brown sugar

½ cup white sugar

1 teaspoon vanilla essence

2 eggs

2 cups standard flour

1 teaspoon baking powder

1 cup chocolate buttons or chopped dark chocolate

Oven temp: 180°C

Method

1. Preheat the oven to 180°C.
2. Put the butter and both lots of sugar in a bowl. Using a whisk, cream it.
3. Add the vanilla and eggs and keep on whisking until it's nice and creamy.
4. Sift in the flour and baking powder, folding with a spoon or spatula.
5. Last but not least add the chocolate and fold it in.
6. Plop dessertspoonsful of the dough onto a greased or lined baking tray.
7. Bake for about 15 minutes.

Suggestion

● Ice cream cookie sandwiches make a great dessert for the kids or a treat for a birthday party. They're as easy as they sound and because these cookies are chewy in the middle they're perfect for this:
   Spoon some ice cream onto the flat side of a chocolate chip cookie. Press another cookie down on top of it. Serve up the 'sandwich' on a plate with a knife and fork.

BROWNIES

WHEN MY OLD FRIEND Dave the Scotsman heard about my penchant for baking, he mocked me mercilessly for about 10 minutes. Suddenly the laughter stopped and, with furrowed brow and piercing eye, he said, 'I reckon I could get you a recipe or two.' And he did, via his friend Jude who gave me this beautiful brownie recipe that has subsequently been made and eaten in our house many times.

 THE KEY: Brownies should be cracked and hard on the outside and gooey in the middle and the way to achieve that is by using brown sugar.

Degree of Difficulty: 2   **Makes** 16

Ingredients

200 g butter   *1 cup standard flour*
½ cup cocoa   *2 eggs, beaten*
2 cups brown sugar   *icing sugar*
1 tsp vanilla essence

Oven temp: 190°C

Method

1. Preheat the oven to 190°C.
2. Melt the butter and cocoa together in a pot. Be careful not to let the mixture boil and keep stirring it.
3. Take the pot off the stove and add the brown sugar. Stir well.
4. Stir in the vanilla, sift in the flour and add the beaten eggs. Mix well. Pour the mixture into a Swiss roll tin lined with baking paper.
5. Bake for 25 minutes. Leave to cool in the tin, sprinkle with sifted icing sugar and then cut into squares, oblongs, triangles or whatever.

MARS BAR BUBBLE SQUARE

A FEW YEARS AGO a woman I work with brought a tiny recipe book into the office. It was a fundraiser (great idea, by the way) put together by parents of the school her kids went to. This recipe was the stand-out one for me. It's very quick and easy, great for children's parties – and the little blokes and blokettes in your house can have some fun helping you make them. You only need three-and-a-half Mars Bars so give yourself a treat and eat the leftover half while you're putting the recipe together.

THE KEY: The caramel stuff in the Mars Bars doesn't melt as well as everything else, but with some dedicated stirring the whole lot will eventually go gluggy.

Degree of Difficulty: 1   **Makes** about 24 squares

Ingredients
  3½ Mars Bars
  75 g butter
  3 cups rice bubbles

Method
1. Chop the Mars Bars into bite-size pieces. Put them in a pot with the butter over a low heat and gently stir until they've melted.
2. Pour in the rice bubbles and stir them through until well mixed.
3. Turn out the mixture into a shallow tin. Pack it down good and tight and of an even thickness.
4. Stick it in the fridge for at least 1 hour until it goes hard and then cut it up into whatever-sized slices you feel like scoffing.

TAN SQUARE

PICTURE A COUNTRY road that curls through the mountainous South Island of New Zealand. There are sheep in the foothills and snow covers the higher peaks. A mate and I were guiding our noisy Cortina along a road just like this, hungry enough to be looking at each other in a way that two blokes really shouldn't when we came across a café.

Actually, the word 'café' might not be doing this place justice. The sign outside was hand-painted as were most of the labels inside that identified the food and I doubt the folks in the kitchen had ever travelled further than the front door. But let me tell you, when we bit into the tan square I believe we heard angels from on high. It was that good. We had a few more slices each and as soon as I got home I hunted down a recipe. It just so happened my Mum had one.

THE KEY: Like the Guns'n'Roses song says, just a little patience. Take your time working the butter into the dough properly otherwise your pinwheels will be uneven.

REVIEWS

Brad: *The girls at work liked it so much last week I am making them another one this week. I doubled the caramel and put milk choc chips on top as well as the shortbread.*
I McLintock: *My mum made this regularly with roughly crushed brazil nuts thru it just so yummy (could use any other nut) cheers.*
Jeff: *I let these cool and turned around to see two left for me – bro' in law and wife scoffed almost all of them. Better than ones I have paid good money for in cafés.*

Degree of Difficulty: 3   **Makes** 16 squares

Ingredients

Base:
150 g butter, softened

75 g sugar

½ teaspoon vanilla essence

275 g standard flour

Filling:
4 tablespoons golden syrup

6 tablespoons condensed milk

6 tablespoons butter

Oven temp: 180°C

Method

1. Preheat the oven to 180°C.
2. Cream the butter, sugar and vanilla essence.
3. Sift in the flour and stir through.
4. Press three-quarters of the mixture into a greased or lined 20 cm square tin and set the rest aside.
5. Combine the golden syrup, condensed milk and second measure of butter in a pot. Bring the mixture to the boil over a low heat, stirring all the time, then leave it to cool.
6. Spread the filling over the base mixture already in the tin. Then crumble the remaining base mixture over the top.
7. Bake for about 30 minutes.

ANZAC BISCUITS

THERE IS NO BLOKIER biscuit than the Anzac. Because these cookies were born of war-time circumstances, they were made to last so they could be sent from home to be eaten in the trenches. But their country of origin remains in dispute with Australian, New Zealand and Scots bakers all claiming to have come up with them first.

The Anzac recipe that we've come to know over the years has been slightly modified here with the addition of a little flavour through the raisins and, if you make them right, a delicious chewy centre.

THE KEY: It's about getting it mixed and into the oven pretty smartly after you've added the baking soda. You need to get a little rise out of these particular Anzacs.

REVIEWS

Virginia : *These rock! They are easy to make and are yum!*
Sandra : *I made these on Anzac day (funny that) and I have to say I got rave reviews from my man and my best friend. De-lic-ious . . . great with a hot cup of tea.*
Steve: *Just right for the kids' lunches. Shaped them by hand. Easier than that spoon and floured-fork girly stuff.*

Degree of Difficulty: 2   **Makes** 12–14

Ingredients

½ cup standard flour

½ cup sugar

½ cup coconut

¾ cup rolled oats

½ cup raisins or sultanas, chopped

100 g butter

2 tablespoons golden syrup

½ teaspoon baking soda

2 tablespoons boiling water

Oven temp: 160°C

Method

1. Preheat the oven to 160°C.
2. Line a baking tray with greased baking paper.
3. In a bowl sift the flour with the sugar, coconut, rolled oats and raisins.
4. Melt the butter and golden syrup together in a pot over a low heat.
5. Dissolve the baking soda in the boiling water and add it to the pot with the butter and syrup.
6. Stir the wet stuff into the dry stuff.
7. Put tablespoonsful of mixture 3–4 cm apart on the lined baking tray. Flatten each blob with a floured fork.
8. Bake for about 15 minutes or until golden.

AFGHANS

ONE OF THE FIRST THINGS I ever baked on the telly was afghans. Now, because I'm a bloke, I tried to be a smart so-and-so and fancy up the icing by piping it on. Minutes before we went to air, there I am with the camera operator and floor manager telling me we're nearly set, asking if I'm ready while I'm fiddling around with a piping bag, fingers covered in chocolate which is getting softer by the second under the lights. There's a bit of panic setting in. So I pipe a thick circle on each one, chuck them on a plate and Bob's your Auntie's second husband.

Which is when the host smiles at me and says, 'That looks like dog do. Three, two, one . . . you're on'.

The finished product should be a delicious soft chocolate cookie wih plenty of crunch that fills the cavern of your mouth like a spoonful of polyfiller.

By the way, I don't put walnuts on mine; but what you do with yours in the privacy of your own home is up to you.

 Don't overbake them. In fact, slightly undercooked is far better as a burnt bottom will kill the taste.

Note *

You can use whatever combination of cereals you like just as long as the total ends up being 2 cups, around a half of which should not be too dry and crunchy. For example, I sometimes use one-and-a-half cups of apricot-flavoured Double Crunch and half a cup of desiccated coconut. But if you try making them with, say, 2 cups of muesli, they'll come out too crunchy. Peter learned this lesson the hard way.

Degree of Difficulty: 2   **Makes** 14–16

Ingredients

200 g butter, softened
½ cup sugar
1¼ cups standard flour
¼ cup cocoa
1 cup crushed Weetbix
1 cup fruity light and tasty-type cereal

Oven temp:
180°C

Method

1. Preheat the oven to 180°C.
2. Using a fork, cream the butter and sugar. Sift in the flour and cocoa and mix well.
3. Fold in the two different types of cereal.* (See note page 30)
4. Spoon round blobs of the mixture onto a greased baking tray and press each one gently with a fork.
5. Bake for about 15 minutes.
6. When they are cool, ice with chocolate icing (see page 161).

CITRUS SHORTBREAD

JUST ON THIS SIDE of the New Year a joker named Brian and I went diving for crayfish up the road and round the corner from McLeod's Bay. Brian's a good man, and a diver of significant experience, so we were pretty confident.

It's not worth wasting your precious time relating how many we caught, or what happened to the weight belt as I was trying to get back into the boat, or how Brian saved the day by going back down 50-odd feet to get it. What's important is that, in the absence of any actual crays and because Brian was so exhausted after saving the belt and a catch bag that went astray as we were surfacing, I volunteered (under duress) to bake dessert. This is what I made. There's little in this world easier than shortbread and the citrus adds a whole lot.

 You could press this into a tin and bake it like a square, but I far prefer to roll it, slice it and make biscuits.

Suggestions

- *If you're not into citrus, add about three-quarters of a cup of currants.*
- *Make them slightly smaller. Whip up some vanilla butter icing (see page 163) and use it to sandwich together the flat sides of the biscuits. Hey presto, citrus yo-yos!*

Degree of Difficulty: 1   **Makes** 24 (approx)

Ingredients

300 g butter
1 cup icing sugar
3 cups standard flour
rind of 1 lemon plus a little juice

Oven temp:
180°C

Method

1. Preheat the oven to 180°C.
2. Line a baking tray with greased baking paper.
3. Cream the butter and icing sugar.
4. Sift in the flour.
5. Add the lemon rind and a tiny squeeze of juice.
6. Roll the dough into a long even sausage.
7. Press the ends of the sausage in gently (so they're flush rather than rounded) and slice off biscuits each about 5 mm wide. Put them on the tray but not too close together; they'll spread a little, but not a lot.
8. Bake for about 15–20 minutes or until the shortbread is just golden.

CHOCOLATE SHORTBREAD

NEWS FLASH: some pregnant women get cravings.

For some reason, when my wife was pregnant with our son, she had a fairly constant urge to eat chocolate. This is only surprising because she's not normally one to display a sweetness of tooth.

Here's another big surprise: some pregnant women are prone to sudden mood swings. Not my wife, though. Not usually, at least. For the most part, even in my most ignorant or self-absorbed moments, I had made it through our marriage so far unscathed. There was one day, however, that I fell short of the mark. She had asked for something sweet and chocolatey, but we were out of cocoa, so I made her some shortbread instead. I delivered it into her thinking what a lucky gal she was and how well she'd done marrying me.

Next thing I was on the receiving end of 'the look', the kind of withering stare that can melt a Bloke.

'I said chocolate,' was all she uttered. I went and got some cocoa and started again. It worked. She loved them. Phew!

 Check them just before the 15 minutes is up. If they go darker brown they're overdone.

Suggestion

- *Our mate Phil reckons another way to make this is to leave out the cocoa and fold about three-quarters of a cup of dark chocolate drops or chips into the creamed butter and sugar.*

Degree of Difficulty: 2   **Makes** 16

Ingredients

200 g butter
100 g caster sugar
2 cups standard flour
7 teaspoons cocoa
pinch of salt
icing sugar for dusting

Oven temp: 180°C

Method

1. Preheat the oven to 180°C.
2. Put the butter in a biggish bowl and soften either in a bain marie (see page 14) or in the microwave. Use an electric beater to whip it up into a creamy texture. Tip in the sugar and keep beating until it's fluffy.
3. Sift in the flour, cocoa and salt and work them through the buttery cream with a wooden spoon until you end up with a ball of dough.
4. Get your hands in there and give it a few seconds of kneading, but not too much!
5. Press the dough into a greased 20–23 cm cake tin until it forms a nice even layer. Pierce the top with a fork a few times.
6. Bake for 15–20 minutes.
7. Once it's out of the oven and cooled, cut it up into triangles and dust with icing sugar.

CHOCOLATE WEETBIX SLICE

THIS STUFF not only tastes good, but all that fibre has to be good for you.

I do not wish to speak ill of Weetbix – or any of the copycat wheat biscuits – but the fact is these days I never eat the things for breakfast because I remember all too well having to down them every single day of my childhood. Weetbix with cold milk, Weetbix with hot milk, crushed Weetbix with boiling water and sugar, whole Weetbix with butter and jam . . . once we even tried Weetbix with peanut butter spread on top. I say once because it's a combination that glued our mouths shut for a week. The point is this: the best way to enjoy Weetbix now is in a slice with chocolate icing.

 THE KEY: You can mess around with the chocolate you use but far and away the best result is achieved with good quality dark chocolate.

Suggestions

- *Here's a really delicious alternative. Instead of putting the chocolate in the slice, you can put it on the slice – in which case leave the chocolate out of the ingredients and replace it with 2 teaspoons of cocoa. You might also try adding half a cup of sultanas for a bit of extra flavour.*
- *Ice the slice with chocolate icing (see page 161). Before the icing cools, throw a layer of desiccated coconut over the top.*

Degree of Difficulty: 2   Makes 16

Ingredients

1 cup standard flour (sifted)

2½ Weetbix, crushed to smithereens

½ cup brown sugar, well packed

1 teaspoon baking powder

½ cup dark chocolate, broken into small pieces

130g butter, melted

Oven temp: 180°C

Method

1. Preheat the oven to 180°C.
2. Throw everything except the butter into a bowl and give it a good mix.
3. Pour the melted butter in and stir until really well combined.
4. Press into a 20 cm square tin or baking dish.
5. Bake for about 25 minutes.

REVIEWS

Greg: *Make a double batch next time at least then it might last longer!*

Blanche: *Fabulous slice . . . stuff all ingredients, easy to make and tastes great!*

GINGER CRUNCH

THE GREATEST THINGS in my opinion to have come out of the tiny island nation of New Zealand are:

Sir Ed Hillary, the All Blacks, the *Lord of the Rings* movies, the Hamilton Jetboat and ginger crunch.

Even the almighty internet couldn't give me the exact origins of this incredible edible, but it does appear to be a New Zealand creation. I'd like to know who came up with it. Possibly it was just something Colin Meads stumbled upon one day while beating up errant English rugby players. Red-haired ones. Can't you see him rumbling toward one of them calling out, 'Hey Ginger,' *crunch*!

 THE KEY: Use a bigger tin if you prefer it thinner and more crunchy or a smaller tin if you like very thick icing.

Suggestion

- *If you want, you can sprinkle the icing with any number of things including chopped nuts or chocolate chips.*

REVIEWS

Teamo: *'No matter how bad I'm baking it always looks and tastes nice.'*
Kylie: *'Comes out perfect every time.'*

Degree of Difficulty: 3   **Makes** 16

Ingredients

Base:
125 g butter

¼ cup sugar

1 teaspoon baking powder

1 cup standard flour

1 teaspoon ground ginger

Icing:
2 tablespoons softened butter

2 teaspoons ground ginger

2 tablespoons golden syrup

2–3 teaspoons water

2 cups icing sugar

Oven temp: 180°C

Method

1. Preheat the oven to 180°C.
2. Line a 21 x 21 cm square tin with greased baking paper or tinfoil.
3. Make the base first. Chop up the butter and zap it for 30-odd seconds in the microwave on a low setting (you don't want it to melt; just nice and soft).
4. Mix in the sugar using a whisk, then stir in the other dry ingredients until it forms a dry dough.
5. Press the dough evenly into the tin and bake for about 10 minutes or until the top turns a wee bit brown.
6. Make the icing while the base is baking.
7. Combine the butter, ginger, golden syrup and water in a pot. Melt over a low heat, gently stirring, until it's smooth.
8. Sift in the icing sugar and stir with a fork until it's completely mixed in.
9. Take the base out of the oven. While it's still warm, cover it with an even layer of icing.
10. Chuck the whole lot in the fridge and let it cool for a couple of hours, then remove it from the tin and chop it up.

GIANT GINGER COOKIES
(Brendan Tourelle)

IF BAKING WAS A SPORT, Brendan Tourelle would be our paralympic representative. He's a legend in the kitchen and works hard helping folk at a place called Sailability. He told me that a few years ago he used to make goodwill visits to a prison where one of the inmates (let's call her 'Mrs S') passed the time helping in the kitchen. Mrs S baked these cookies for Brendan, partly to thank him for the time he'd spent there, and partly for the file he smuggled in.

The inmates in that prison must have liked to spice things up a bit because these cookies pack a punch. (All puns in this story intended!)

 THE KEY: Bake them on two separate trays; one high in the oven and one low. About halfway through the baking switch them around.

Note
Freezing the dough for 20 minutes makes it easier to work with. Cookies can be baked up to two days ahead; store in an airtight container at room temperature.

Oven temp:
180°C

Degree of Difficulty: 2   **Makes** 12

Ingredients

2½ cups standard flour (sifted)

2¼ teaspoons baking soda

½ teaspoon salt

1 tablespoon ground ginger

½ teaspoon mixed spice

½ teaspoon black pepper

150 g butter at room temperature

½ cup brown sugar, well packed

½ cup white sugar plus ⅓ cup
   for coating

6 tablespoons molasses

1 large egg

Method

1. Preheat the oven to 180°C.
2. Line 2 baking trays with greased baking paper and set aside.
3. In a decent-size bowl whisk together the flour, baking soda, salt, ginger, mixed spice, and pepper.
4. Cream the butter, brown sugar and the first measure of white sugar until the mixture is light and fluffy.
5. Beat in the molasses and egg.
6. Stir the combined dry ingredients into the creamed butter until just combined.
7. Flatten into a disk, wrap in plastic clingfilm, and stick in the freezer for 20 minutes.
8. Divide the chilled dough into 12 balls and roll each one in the remaining sugar to coat.
9. Place the balls on the lined trays with plenty of room in between them (this is why you need 2 trays). Flatten each one with a fork and sprinkle with the sugar still left in the bowl.
10. Bake for about 12–15 minutes until just brown, switching trays halfway through.

MARSHMALLOW SLICE
(James Dunne)

A COUPLE OF YEARS back I was invited to help judge a Blokes' Bake-off at a financial services company. The competition was fierce and the standard of baking extremely impressive, but the big winner on the day came as something of a surprise. A quiet bloke who'd gone to a lot of trouble perfecting a very pink slice. Not blokey, I grant you, but the thing was spectacular. The quiet bloke's name was James and he told me he got the recipe from the wife of one of the other guys in the competition. The other guy came second.

Crikey, James! That's called cutting your mate's lunch! Worth it, though. Great slice. (By the way, the other bloke in this whole sordid-but-tasty affair was Neil – his blueberry muffins are featured on page 48.)

THE KEY: Pour about a third of the icing sugar into the egg white before you start beating and add the rest of the sugar bit by bit as you go. You know the egg whites are done when you lift the beater out and the peaks of white stand up.

Degree of Difficulty: 5   **Makes** 16–18

Ingredients

Base:

250 g butter, softened

1 cup sugar

1 egg

1 teaspoon baking powder

1¾ cups standard flour

Marshmallow:

2 cups water

2 cups sugar

4 tablespoons powdered gelatine

2 egg whites

2 cups icing sugar

2 drops red food colouring
  (or whatever colour you like)

½ teaspoon vanilla essence

2 tablespoons desiccated coconut

Oven temp:
180°C

Method

1. Preheat the oven to 180°C.
2. Make the base first. Cream the butter and sugar.
3. Add the egg and sifted dry ingredients and mix everything together.
4. Press the mixture (don't be too heavy-handed) evenly into a 23 cm square tin.
5. Bake for about 25–30 minutes or until golden brown.
6. To make the marshmallow, combine the water, first measure of sugar and the gelatine in a decent-sized pot over a medium heat until the contents dissolve. Turn up the heat and boil the mixture for 8 minutes. Add the food colouring and vanilla and set aside to cool.
7. In a separate bowl beat the egg whites until stiff, slowly adding the icing sugar as you go.
8. Slowly pour the warm gelatine mixture into the egg whites and keep beating for a few minutes with an electric mixer. The marshmallow mixture should become very thick.
9. Pour immediately over the base. Sprinkle with coconut.
10. Stick the tin in the fridge to cool and set.

WHITE CHRISTMAS

HERE ARE THE TOP five things I love about Christmas. You might think it's not a very Christmassy list and that I should probably include 'time with family' or 'the joy of giving', etc. But here's what I really love:

- Time off work.
- Watching my son open his presents.
- Eating ham and pavlova until my stomach just can't hold any more, then squeezing a little more in for luck.
- Leaning back after lunch, loosening my belt, possibly belching and generally chilling out.
- This stuff.

A woman named Shirley from St Oran's College taught me how to make White Christmas and it comes in handy – not only as a delicious snack for the family, but also as a DIY gift that you can wrap and hand over to the folks you like.

THE KEY: It's all about the mixing. After it's been in the fridge the Kremelta can sink to the bottom if it hasn't been mixed properly. Mix it really thoroughly to minimise this problem.

Suggestion

- *Here's an idea for Christmas. Slice the White Christmas into smallish squares, whip up a batch of truffles (see page 138) and wrap a few of each along with some cherries or berries in cellophane or put them in a gift box.*

Degree of Difficulty: 2   **Makes** 20

Ingredients
250 g Kremelta
1 cup desiccated coconut
1 cup powdered milk
¾ cup icing sugar
1 cup dried fruit (I like to use chopped apricots and sultanas)
1½ cups rice bubbles
½ teaspoon vanilla essence

Method
1. Line a sponge roll tin with baking paper (no need to grease).
2. Melt the Kremelta in the microwave or over a low heat.
3. In a separate bowl mix together all the dry ingredients, then pour the melted Kremelta over them. Mix well and press the whole lot into the prepared tin. Stick it in the fridge for at least 1 hour to set before slicing it into fingers. Keep it in the fridge.

Muffins
and Scones

Understanding the Lingo

Grease. (v) pron: a) GREE-s or b) Gr-EE-zz

a) *A film in which Olivia Newton-John appears wearing a very tight leather outfit and singing with the always cool John Travolta.*

b) *The stuff you apply to bearings to reduce friction so they move more freely.*

c) *To compliment someone unnecessarily for personal gain.*

GREASING is possibly the most important part of the prep work before you bake. It means coating the inside or top of a tin or tray with butter or oil. It's often best to line whatever you're using with baking paper or foil first and then grease that. Spray oil is the fastest way to grease, but I'm a fan of good old-fashioned butter as it adds flavour. You can, with cakes and loaves, sprinkle sugar or dust the butter with flour. If you do that, tip out the excess. See 'Top tips' on page 13 for more hints on greasing.

❝Yes, I know the Muffin Man.❞
Lord Farquaad, Shrek

**❝On Wednesday he goes shopping
And has buttered scones for tea.❞**
The Lumberjack Song, Monty Python

BLUEBERRY MUFFINS
(Neil Carter)

ON PAGE 42 you'll see a story about a baking competition with an extra edge. The thing is, the guy who won it (James) was gifted his recipe by the wife of the guy who came second. But Neil (the runner-up) is a classy bloke and to this day refuses to say a bad word about James. 'Nah, it's okay,' he told me. 'He might have won with a nice pink slice, but I still got the girl.'

You know your priorities, Neil. Outside of the best blueberry muffins known to man, that's what we really like about you.

THE KEY: Keep the wet and dry stuff separate until the last minute and make sure the oven is good and hot before the muffins go in. You want to get a crispy shell with delicious soft muffin inside.

REVIEWS

Kylie: *Great muffin recipe – I now use it as my basic muffin recipe and then add whatever we have at the time. Yummy!*

Tony: *Never made muffins before although I cook every day. Absolutely brilliant and earned me a lot of brownie points.*

Glenis: *Nice, easy recipe to make. Lovely muffins.*

Brett: *The sugar and cinnamon topping is excellent. Highly recommended.*

Evan: *These are great, I don't have much luck with muffins and these came out perfect. Very quick and easy to make.*

Mika: *Made these yesterday and they were perfect! Best ones I've ever had! Everyone thought they were 10/10! Soft in the middle, crispy on the outside and delicious!*

Degree of Difficulty: 3   **Makes** 12 regular muffins

Ingredients

2 cups standard flour

4 teaspoons baking powder

½ cup sugar

1 egg

1 teaspoon vanilla essence

1 cup milk

100 g butter, melted

1½ cups frozen blueberries

cinnamon and icing sugar for dusting

Oven temp: 200°C

Method

1. Preheat the oven to 200°C.
2. Combine the dry ingredients (sifting flour) in a large bowl.
3. Grab a separate bowl and mix the egg, vanilla, milk and butter.
4. Stir the frozen blueberries into the flour mixture, then stir in the wet stuff.
5. Put the mixture into the muffin trays and bake for about 20 minutes, depending on the size of the muffins. Big ones will need a little longer.
6. Dust the tops with cinnamon and icing sugar when they're done.

CINNAMON PINWHEELS

NOT SO LONG AGO I was invited to a barbecue with a bunch of blokes who cook and bake for a living. The instructions were to bring something for dessert. I felt like a duck on the first day of hunting season. I mean, most of these jokers were head chefs and pastry chefs at big, flash joints.

I reckoned these pinwheels would be the way to go – they look fancy, but they don't take long and fresh out of the oven they're hard to beat for taste.

Here's what happened: when the cloth was lifted from the dessert table my pinwheels were the first things to disappear. I'm not saying they were better than Pierre's éclairs, just that they were picked up faster. Ah, what the heck. I am saying they were better and Pierre can come and sort me out if he's up to it.

 THE KEY: Take your time working the butter into the dough properly, otherwise your pinwheels will be uneven.

TOP TIPS

Make sure the dough is rolled out evenly or the cookies will come out looking up and down and all over the place.

When you're kneading, remember that your end result has to be square, so try and get the dough into a squarish sort of shape right from the start. It'll make life easier.

Suggestion

- *Ice them with vanilla icing (see page 160) dribbled in zig-zag lines.*

Degree of Difficulty: 3   **Makes** 10–12

Ingredients

Dough:

2 cups standard flour

4 teaspoons baking powder

1 teaspoon salt

2 tablespoons sugar

100 g butter (cut into chunks)

¾ cup milk

Filling:

75 g butter, softened

¾ cup brown sugar, well packed

1 heaped tablespoon cinnamon

½ cup raisins or sultanas
 (optional)

Oven temp: 220°C

Method

1. Preheat the oven to 220°C.
2. Make the dough first. Combine the sifted dry ingredients.
3. Chuck in the butter and mix it with your fingers. Go on – get your hands dirty! The mix should feel like a bit like soft breadcrumbs.
4. Add the milk and stir through until the dough is soft. It'll almost look a bit too wet – but don't sweat it.
5. Turn out the dough onto a floured surface and knead it with the heel of your hand. Keep on rolling and then working it until it's a nice soft (almost pastry-like) dough.
6. Roll out the dough into a flat square about 30 by 30 cm.
7. Now it's time to get the filling together. Spread butter out over the surface of the dough.
8. Mix together the brown sugar and cinnamon – and dried fruit if you're using it – and sprinkle over the top.
9. Roll it all up – carefully. Seal it with a bit of melted butter. Cut into 2.5 cm wide pieces and put them, flat, on a baking tray lined with a sheet of baking paper.
10. Bake for about 15 minutes.

SHANDY SCONES

I REMEMBER as a young bloke trekking through an area too remote even to be referred to as 'the middle of nowhere'. When you go out the back of beyond, somewhere north of the black stump, you're probably still an hour's walk through scrub to get to this place.

I was there with a man named Snow; wire thin, all bone and sinew and calluses. He wasn't a big man, but he was a local legend in wood-chopping circles. I was there to watch and learn and lug some of the cut blocks onto the ute. At the end of that long day Snow sat back in his rickety chair and took a long, thirsty pull from a glass of shandy.

Now, go ahead and tell me that shandy's a sheila's drink – because if it's good enough for Snow, then it's good enough for these scones.

 THE KEY: Go easy on the kneading (otherwise they'll be tough). Try and just use your fingers, not the palm of your hand.

Suggestion

This is just a basic recipe – but probably the world's easiest and most versatile – so from here you can go to town if you feel so inclined. Try the following variations:

- *Use beer instead of shandy (if you can bear to part with it).*
- *Use lemonade instead of beer (which will solve the earlier problem).*
- *If it's beer you use, sprinkle a little cheese over before you fold the dough. Tasty.*
- *If it's all lemonade, add half a cup of raisins or currants to the mix. Eat them warm with the classic jam and whipped cream combination. It's a stunner.*

Degree of Difficulty: 2   Makes 8–10

Ingredients

3 cups standard flour
5 teaspoons baking powder
1 teaspoon salt
1 cup cream
1 cup shandy (50% beer, 50% lemonade)

Oven temp: 220°C

Method

1. Preheat the oven to 220°C.
2. Sift the dry ingredients into a bowl.
3. Make a well in the middle and pour in the cream.
4. Gently mix it all together, then pour in the shandy (you can quietly work through the leftover beer while you're working).
5. Turn out the dough onto a floured bench. Gently knead (remember to use only your fingers), then form the dough into a squarish shape about 1.5 cm thick.
6. Fold over the dough – but don't knead it any more (the reason for folding it is because it'll be easier to pull the scones apart when they're ready to eat).
7. Cut the dough into the size scones you want and chuck them on a baking tray that's greased or lined with a sheet of baking paper.
8. Bake for about 12–15 minutes (the bigger they are, the longer they'll take).

APPLE AND SULTANA MUFFINS

BACK IN THE EARLY DAYS of what has become my baking hobby I had a little trouble with muffin moistness – or rather, the lack of it. The solution came to me one evening in a flash of blinding brilliance as I was hunkered down in the smallest room in our house; it's where I do my best thinking. The idea, it seemed to me, was to make a muffin with a little fruit in it. And being a fan of the apple and cinnamon combination of flavours I gave this one a crack, as it were. Folks seemed to like it.

THE KEY: As with most muffins, it's about knowing when to stop folding. Get to the point where the flour is just mixed through and that's it. Enough! Even if you want to give it one more go just for luck, don't.

TOP TIP

Muffin cups should be about three-quarters full. That gives them plenty of room to rise, but not that much that they'll spill out all over the place.

REVIEWS

Cathy: *Wow! These are wonderful, and a 'must bake'. Next day reheat a little in the microwave – delicious.*
Te Rina: *Ten out of ten. Delicious and easy to make!*
Liam: *Fantastic recipe! The whole family enjoyed them. They are so easy to make. I will definitely bake them again.*
Louise: *This is a great recipe. I've also made it using banana and choc chips instead of the apple and sultanas.*

Degree of Difficulty: 3   **Makes** 12 regular or 6 man-sized muffins.

Ingredients

1 egg

¼ cup cooking oil

½ cup sugar

1 cup milk

2 cups standard flour

4 teaspoons baking powder

2 teaspoons cinnamon

1¼ cups chopped apple and sultanas (about half of each in the mix)

Oven temp: 200°C

Method

1. Preheat the oven to 200°C.
2. Beat the egg and oil together until it gets to the stage your wife would describe as 'light and fluffy'.
3. Pour in the sugar and milk and keep on beating.
4. Sift in the flour, baking powder and cinnamon and fold it through using a flat knife or spatula.
5. As you're folding, add the chopped fruit.
6. Spoon the mix into a greased muffin tray.
7. Bake for about 25 minutes.

APRICOT YOGHURT SCONES

DO YOU REMEMBER all those things your parents used to tell you with the aim of either stopping you from doing something or getting you to do it more often?

Here are some examples:

- When you're pulling a face: 'If the wind changes, you'll be stuck like that forever.'
- When you won't eat your crusts: 'They'll make your hair curly.'
- When fishing out lint from your belly button: 'If you keep playing with that your bum will fall off.'
- The always useful: 'Watching too much TV will give you square eyes.'
- Once I was eating an apricot and accidentally swallowed the stone. It went down hard and almost jammed in my throat. Then, just to add insult to injury, my mother told me that I was in trouble. 'Well, that's it,' she said. 'Now an apricot tree will grow in your tummy.' I worried about that for days.

THE KEY: Pretend you work at the Post Office and a parcel has come through marked 'Fragile'. Hmm, scratch that. OK, pretend you work as an airline baggage handler and . . . nope, still no good. Just handle with care.

Suggestion

- *Once they're done, and while they're still warm, top them with butter and apricot jam, or jam and whipped cream.*

Degree of Difficulty: 3   **Makes** 8–10

Ingredients

3 cups standard flour
5 teaspoons baking powder
1 teaspoon salt
75 g butter, chopped
¾ cup chopped dried apricots
1 pot (150 g) apricot yoghurt
1¼ cups milk

Oven temp:
220°C

Method

1. Preheat the oven to 220°C.
2. Sift the flour and baking powder into a bowl with the salt.
3. Using your fingers, squeeze the butter into the flour until the mixture is like rough breadcrumbs.
4. Stir in the chopped apricots.
5. Make a well in the middle and pour in the yoghurt and milk.
6. Mix gently with a spatula, just until it's thoroughly mixed.
7. Turn out the dough onto a floured bench and gently flatten it with the heel of your hand before shaping into a square about 2 cm thick.
8. Cut scones into the size you want and chuck them on a greased or lined baking tray.
9. Bake for 12–15 minutes (the bigger they are, the longer they'll take).

SULTANA ROCK CAKES

HERE'S my list of the world's greatest rocks:

- Rock'n'roll
- Chris Rock
- Alcatraz
- 30 Rock
- The Rock of Gibraltar
- Dwayne 'The Rock' Johnson
- Ayers Rock
- The Hard Rock Café

You choose if – and where – on that list these wee gems belong.

THE KEY: Not too much milk. Add a wee splash (i.e., not all at once) and mix it through, then a little more until the floury dryness turns into a thick dough. But that's all.

Suggestion

- *Our mate Brogan adds chocolate chips but ditches the cinnamon.*

Degree of Difficulty: 2   **Makes** about 22–24

Ingredients

1 cup standard flour

1½ teaspoons baking powder

½ teaspoon cinnamon

50 g butter

¼ cup sugar

½ cup chopped sultanas

1 egg, whisked

2 tablespoons milk

Oven temp:
200°C

Method

1. Preheat the oven to 200°C.
2. Sift the flour, baking powder and cinnamon into a bowl.
3. Melt the butter slowly over a low heat and then stir it into the flour with a fork until the mixture is like coarse breadcrumbs. If it's lumpy – keep stirring.
4. Add the sugar and sultanas followed by the whisked egg and milk (remember – not too much milk).
5. Get a good heaped teaspoon of the mixture, ball it up gently in your hands and plonk it onto a greased baking tray. Repeat until the mixture is all used.
6. Bake for about 10–12 minutes.

FRUIT BUTTERMILK SCONES
(Annabelle White)

WHEN I FIRST got into this baking lark one of the most encouraging people was a woman named Annabelle White. You've probably heard of Annabelle; she's the Cuddly Cook from any number of TV shows, radio programmes and with approximately a brazillian (more than a billion) books to her name.

Annabelle is hilarious on air and in person; she is generous with her time and advice and she's serious about her baking. She graciously allowed me to use this recipe, which I asked for on the basis that it's so damn good.

THE KEY: According to Annabelle, best results come from using good quality ingredients and following the instructions (in other words, the order in which things happen *does* matter).

REVIEWS

> **Vanda:** *Way nicer than with ordinary milk. If you like them sweet add 70 g sugar. The wife can't get enough of them!*
>
> **Sandra:** *Four women, 12 scones, morning tea . . . all gone. Say no more, except bl**dy delicious!*

Degree of Difficulty: 3   **Makes** 10

Ingredients

3 cups self-raising flour
1 heaped teaspoon baking powder
pinch of salt
70 g butter, chilled
1 cup dried fruit (a combination of chopped
  apricots and raisins is delicious)
1–1½ cups buttermilk

Oven temp:
230°C

Method

1. Preheat the oven to 230°C.
2. Chuck the sifted flour, baking powder and salt in a bowl.
3. Grate in the cold butter and squeeze through with your fingers as quickly and as lightly as possible – the less you handle it the better.
4. When the mixture is fully integrated and resembles fine breadcrumbs, add the dried fruit and the buttermilk (but give the container a good shake first), stirring in the buttermilk with a flat knife or spatula. Keep the mixture wetter than normal.
5. Place the mixture on a floured bench and gently pat into shape with a few gentle movements – do not knead.
6. Using a sharp knife, cut the dough into pieces and place close together on a lined or greased baking tray.
7. Bake for about 15–18 minutes.

LEMON MUFFINS

WE HAVE A LEMON TREE in the front garden, but as trees go it's something of a lemon. There is also a lemon tree out the back. Technically it belongs to our neighbour, being that it's planted in his soil and he's done all the work getting it to its current state of magnificence. There are, however, branches that hang over our side and some of those branches are adorned with plump, juicy, yellow fruit.

So, and God may strike me down for admitting it in public, every now and then we nick some. The wife and I have done a deal: she does the nicking, and I bake the muffins.

THE KEY: If you bake these for even a couple of minutes too long they'll go dry. Check them after 20 and again after 25 minutes. Gently press the top of one of them and if it bounces back, it's about ready to eat.

Suggestion

- *Make some runny lemon icing with lemon juice and a little icing sugar and drizzle it over the tops. Or, if you can't be bothered with that, just squeeze a little juice over them and sprinkle with sugar. Beautiful.*

REVIEWS

Glen: *Bang on.*
Mike: *Easy to bake, easy to eat. Yum!*
Albert: *Excellent recipe, brought the muffins into work, now they want me to bake at least once a week! Yeah, right!*

Degree of Difficulty: 3   **Makes** 6 big manly-man muffins

Ingredients

2 cups standard flour

1 cup sugar

2 heaped teaspoons baking powder

1 teaspoon salt

zest and juice of 3–4 lemons

100 g butter, melted

2 eggs

Oven temp: 160°C

Method

1. Preheat the oven to 160°C.
2. Grease the muffin tray.
3. Sift the flour, then mix in the other dry ingredients and the grated zest.
4. Pour the lemon juice into a measuring cup and then make up it to a little more than 1 cup (about 275 ml is plenty) using water.
5. In a separate bowl, combine the juice with the melted butter and eggs. Beat the combo until it's good and frothy.
6. Chuck the wet stuff into the dry and fold it through until just combined.
7. Stick it into the prepared muffin tray and bake for about 30 minutes.

CINNAMON SCONES

ONE THING the old man gave me before he left this Earth was his dicky ticker; in other words a bit of potential heart trouble. Actually, what this means is that like most of the population I have a higher than ideal cholesterol level. And it ain't helped by all my baking and eating of delicious treats.

Imagine my delight then – and yours, I hope – when the news that *cinnamon can lower cholesterol* came to hand. Studies show that, apparently, just half a teaspoon a day will do the trick.

At that rate, a couple of these scones every lunchtime is about right. As the band Coup D'état once sang, 'Doctor I like your medicine . . . .'

THE KEY: Although I might be starting to sound like a broken record, just remember that when you're making scones, the idea is to handle them as little as possible.

Suggestion

- *If you're a fan of raisins try adding quarter of a cup to the topping mix. You can then kid yourself that you're making the whole thing even healthier!*

Degree of Difficulty: 3   **Makes** 8–10

Ingredients

2 cups standard flour

4 teaspoons baking powder

½ cup sugar

½ teaspoon salt

50 g butter (chopped)

1 cup milk

Topping:

¼ cup brown sugar, well packed

2 teaspoons cinnamon

Oven temp: 220°C

Method

1. Preheat the oven to 220°C.
2. Sift the flour and baking powder into a bowl with the sugar and salt.
3. Rub the butter in until the mixture looks and feels like rough breadcrumbs.
4. Make a well in the middle and pour in the milk.
5. Mix gently with a spatula just until it's thoroughly mixed.
6. Turn out the dough onto a floured bench.
7. Gently flatten the dough with the heel of your hand and shape it into a large square about 1 cm thick.
8. Sprinkle the topping over the whole lot, then fold over once so the topping is now in the middle.
9. Cut into squares and place on a greased or lined baking tray.
10. Bake for about 12 minutes (the bigger they are, the longer they'll take).

RASPBERRY AND WHITE CHOCOLATE MUFFINS

WAY UP HIGH, in an otherwise unremarkable office building in the country's capital city, sits a man named Clark* who, by day, goes quietly about his business. But as the sun sets over the western hills of this great city Clark's alter ego emerges. He flings aside his tie, kicks off his shoes and loosens his morals, transforming in mere minutes from mild-mannered account executive to . . . Baker Man! Whenever a dumpling's in danger, wherever a slice is unsafe, if there's a cake crime being cooked up, Baker Man is there.

Rumour has it that Baker Man once used these muffins to save drowning puppies that were being borne down upon by a nuclear warship somewhere in the southern Pacific Ocean. It is not for me to either confirm or deny. What I *will* say is that Clark gave me one of the best recipes I've ever come across for muffins and now I'm giving it to you.

* The name in the story may have been changed to protect the innocent.

THE KEY: Always treat muffins with care. You've probably seen people drop the muffin tray on the bench a couple of times before putting it in the oven. Don't do that. You'll knock the air out of them and they don't appreciate it.

TOP TIP
Save dropping in the berries until the very end so they don't ooze too much colour into the mixture.

Degree of Difficulty: 3   **Makes** about 24 mini muffins

Ingredients

2 cups standard flour

4 teaspoons baking powder

½ cup brown sugar, well packed

½ cup chopped white chocolate or white chocolate chips

½ cup cooking oil

¾ cup milk

2 eggs

1½ cups raspberries, preferably frozen

Oven temp: 200°C

Method

1. Preheat the oven to 200°C.
2. Sift the flour into a bowl with the other dry ingredients and stir with a fork.
3. Chuck the chopped-up chocolate into another bowl along with the oil, milk and eggs and whisk until smooth.
4. Drop the berries into the flour mix, then stir again with a fork.
5. Pour in the smooth oil/egg mixture and fold it through gently and until it's just mixed.
6. Bake in greased muffin trays for about 20 minutes.

BANANA CHOCOLATE CHIP MUFFINS ('Chief')

HATS OFF as a mark of respect please, lads. There's a joker I know with an air of such authority that most of us don't even know his real name. He simply goes by the handle, 'Chief'. Where this nickname came from or how it was bestowed upon him, I've never had the gumption to ask.

But even the Chief has to bow down to someone. Even he must follow orders when they come from higher up. I refer, of course, to his wife. Knowing he was a fellow baker, I asked Chief if he'd be kind enough to share a recipe. He gave it to me in the form of a note that he told me he'd found hidden in his wife's secret cash box. This tells me two things: One, that Chief knows the location of the box and it is not such a secret after all. And two, that this is a good recipe. There was no cash in the box, just this.

 THE KEY: Fold the mixture carefully. Roll your spatula through slowly until the flour is just combined and no more.

Note

If you use too much banana the muffins will become soggy and won't rise as well. But don't tell Chief I said that. He might take it as criticism.

Degree of Difficulty: 3   **Makes** 12 regular muffins

Ingredients

1½ cups standard flour

3 teaspoons baking powder

½ cup sugar

1 cup chocolate chips

2 Weetbix, crushed

1 egg

100 g butter, melted

1 cup milk

1 large or 2 smallish bananas, mashed

Oven temp: 200°C

Method

1. Preheat the oven to 200°C.
2. Sift the flour, baking powder and sugar into a bowl.
3. Stir in the chocolate chips and crushed Weetbix, then make a hole (women call this a 'well') in the middle of the mixture.
4. In a separate bowl, beat the egg and stir in the melted butter along with the milk, then pour this liquid into the well in the dry ingredients.
5. Add the mashed banana, then stir briefly – just enough so that it's mushed together.
6. Bake for about 15–20 minutes.

Cakes *and* Loaves

Understanding the Lingo

Batter. (v) pron: BAD-ah'

a) *The guy you bowl or pitch to.*

b) *What Mike Tyson did to his opponents (See also ear-biter).*

c) *(Similar) Worse than. As in: 'I'm badder than Michael Jackson'.*

OFTEN WHEN baking a cake or loaf you'll see a reference to 'batter', which may seem odd. Really the only difference between a standard cake mixture and a batter is that batter is runny. The gingerbread loaf on page 74 for example is a runny mix that is technically a batter. This is why I've put muffins and cakes in different categories. With muffins you generally have to fold whereas there are plenty of cakes or loaves that need real mixing.

'Let them eat cake.'

Marie Antoinette

'It's a matter of loaf and death, Gromit!'

Wallace, from Wallace and Gromit

BANANA CAKE

WHEN I WAS just an excitable lad of 12 I had something of a crush on one of my Mum's friends. Yes, she was 24 years older than me, but love is blind and I thought I had a shot.

One of my fondest memories is cycling the 5 kilometres into town to spend the afternoon baking banana cake with her. We mixed and folded and iced, our fingers occasionally intertwining along to the Righteous Brothers' soaring harmonies.

Finally we ate the perfect cake whilst the sun shone in the window and the birds sang songs of joy in the eucalyptus tree outside. Although it is possible I'm romanticising the whole thing because I fancied her.

THE KEY: The main trouble folks have with banana cake is that it can come out dry. The way to stop this is by very slightly under-baking it. Drag it out of the oven just before it's done and stick a piece of tin foil over the hot cake, letting it finish slowly.

Suggestion

- *A joker who works at Resene, but wishes to remain anonymous, gave me a recipe for a banana cake free of the health hazards that butter allegedly brings with it. Or, for those who have run out of butter but have oil in the pantry.*
  Instead of 125 g butter, use 125 ml canola oil, sunflower oil or something along those lines. Do not use olive oil, fish oil or motor oil. Mix and cook the same way for the same amount of time.

Degree of Difficulty: 3   **Serves** 10

Ingredients

125 g butter

¾ cup sugar

2 eggs

3–4 smashed bananas

1 teaspoon baking soda

2 tablespoons hot milk

2 cups standard flour

1 teaspoon baking powder

1 teaspoon cinnamon

Oven temp:
180°C

Method

1. Preheat the oven to 180°C.
2. Zap the butter for 30 seconds in the microwave (or until it's soft but not melted) then cream in the sugar.
3. Add the eggs one at a time and keep on beating until it's smooth as a 20-year-old Brazilian model's rear end. Add the smashed bananas and stir through.
4. Separately stir the baking soda into the hot milk until it dissolves and pour the milk into your mixture. Then sift in the dry ingredients.
5. Don't overmix – just fold it all through and then pour it out into the cake tin.
6. Bake for about 45–50 minutes.

GINGERBREAD LOAF

THERE'S GOOD GINGER:

- Boris Becker (tennis bloke)
- Ron Howard (Richie Cunningham and movie bloke)
- Prince Harry (more blokey than his brother Willie)
- That guy from *CSI: Miami*

AND THERE'S HOT GINGER:

- Nicole Kidman
- Gillian Anderson
- Lindsay Lohan

And then there's this: the greatest gingerbread loaf that man has ever tasted! No, I don't think that's overstating it. I am the most dedicated person in the history of the universe to avoid the fatal perils of exaggeration.

THE KEY: Getting it mixed and into the oven pretty smartly after you've added the baking soda. The chemical reaction starts as soon as that soda hits the milk and if you faff around the loaf won't rise as well.

Suggestion

The easiest way to enjoy this is sliced with a little butter on it. Perfect with your daily coffee fix. But for something a little more decadent, try this:

- *Warm a little cream gently over a low heat (how much depends on how many you're feeding).*
  - *Drop a vanilla pod into the cream.*
  - *Keep it on the heat and keep stirring for about 5 minutes.*
  - *Let the cream cool and then whip it, just until it thickens a little.*
  - *Spoon the vanilla cream onto your gingerbread.*

Degree of Difficulty: 3   **Makes** 1 loaf

Ingredients

1 tablespoon white sugar

⅓ cup golden syrup

¾ cup brown sugar, well packed

125 g butter

1 cup standard flour

⅓ cup cornflour

2 teaspoons ground ginger

1½ teaspoons mixed spice

½ cup milk

1 teaspoon baking soda

1 egg, whisked

Oven temp: 160°C

Method

1. Preheat the oven to 160°C.
2. Prep a 20 cm loaf tin by greasing it, then sprinkling white sugar around the base and tipping out the excess.
3. Melt the golden syrup, brown sugar and butter together over a low heat. Don't let them boil.
4. Sift in the flour, cornflour, ginger and spice. Fold it through.
5. Warm the milk in the microwave and stir in the baking soda. Add that as quickly as possible to the mixture.
6. Finally add the egg and give the batter a good stir.
7. Bake for about 50–60 minutes.

Note

The batter may seem runnier than usual by the time you add the egg. Don't worry about it, everything is fine.

LEMON MADEIRA CAKE

ONE OF THE THINGS that bothers me most about the song 'Ironic' by Alanis Morissette is that none of the things she sings about are actually ironic.

Rain on your wedding day? Not ironic.

Ten thousand spoons when all you need is a knife? Not ironic.

Most of them are coincidental, some could be described as crappy luck, but none are ironic. And that, I suppose, makes the whole song kind of ironic and thus the title fits. There are other things that bother me about the song, but none are relevant here.

Quick story: Madeira is a group of islands off the Coast of Portugal. By a quirk of coincidence I have been to Portugal. Madeira is also a kind of fortified wine. I have drunk it. In Portugal! Madeira is also a delicious cake. It's one of the three core cakes that I believe everyone should know how to bake (along with chocolate and banana). I have made and eaten Madeira cake. Thus I am familiar with Madeira in all its forms. But this isn't about me – it's about the cake and helping you to bake it.

Much like the song – none of that is ironic.

 THE KEY: Hold the milk back until after the flour has gone in. And keep an eye on the time. I bake this in a 20 cm tin and it ain't a high-rising cake.

Suggestions

- *Don't throw away the lemon that you've grated the rind from. Squeeze the juice over the top of the cake and then sprinkle with sugar.*
- *This is another great birthday cake for those who might not be into heavy chocolate. Triple the recipe and make it in a decent-sized baking dish or a roasting dish. Because it doesn't rise super high you can cut shapes out of it and build a castle or make a train.*
- *Ice it with colourful lemon icing.*

Degree of Difficulty: 2   **Serves** 8

Ingredients
100 g butter
½ cup sugar
1 egg
zest of 1 lemon
1 cup standard flour
1 teaspoon baking powder
½ cup milk

Oven temp:
180°C

Method
1. Preheat the oven to 180°C.
2. Grease or line a 20 cm round cake tin.
3. In a bowl cream the butter and sugar until smooth.
4. Add the egg and whisk well.
5. Add the lemon rind and stir through.
6. Sift in the flour and baking powder and start to fold.
7. Pour in the milk and stir.
8. Tip it into your prepped tin.
9. Bake for about 40–45 minutes.

VERY BIG CHOCOLATE CAKE

JUST ABOUT EVERYONE I know has a chocolate cake recipe they swear by, and I'm no exception. For a long time I found baking chocolate cake to be something akin to most New Year's Eve parties. That is to say, full of hope and promise but ultimately disappointing (which, coincidentally, is almost word for word how several ex-girlfriends have described our relationship).

I tried plenty of recipes, none of which quite seemed to give me what I wanted. And then I found this. Or rather – it was given to me by my good friend KB. It's not only the best chocolate cake recipe I've ever tried, it's also the easiest. Two thumbs up.

 THE KEY: Add the ingredients in the order they're listed and just keep on beating. The exception to this is the moment you add the cocoa. Just stir that through for a few seconds first. Then beat away again to your heart's content.

Note

This is perfect for birthday cakes because you can cut out the shape you want and still have plenty of cake.

Suggestion

- *Decorate with chocolate butter icing (see page 163).*

Degree of Difficulty: 2   **Serves** 14

Ingredients

2 cups sugar

2 large eggs

1 cup milk

¾ cup cocoa

200 g butter, softened

2 teaspoons baking soda

1½ teaspoons vanilla essence

1 teaspoon salt

3 cups standard flour

4 teaspoons baking powder

1 cup strong hot coffee

Oven temp: 160°C

Method

1. Preheat the oven to 160°C.
2. Line a large baking dish (or roasting dish) with greased baking paper.
3. Get yourself a large bowl and add each ingredient in the order it's given above. It's even easier if you've got a mixing machine. So, beat the sugar and eggs together and then add the milk, beat some more, stir in the cocoa, and beat. And so on. With an automatic mixer, just turn it on and keep adding things.
4. After the coffee's been added and beaten in, you should have a smooth creamy batter.
5. Bake for about 1 hour in a 23 cm cake tin (if you use a larger tin it will not bake as high and will take less time).

NANA'S CHRISTMAS CAKE
(Nigel Bradly)

THE THING you ought to know about Nige is that a group of his close friends know him better as 'Cheeks'. It's not for me to go into the details about who was showing off around a bonfire and which part of his body might have been set alight as a result. The point is that for a doctor he's a fun bloke and always up for a laugh. As luck would have it, he also bakes.

He reckons that the thing with his Nana's recipe is you need to put enough brandy in it to drown a small army – and then cook it months ahead so that by the time the big day rolls round you can get half-cut just by smelling the fumes. His Nana was no alcoholic, mind you. She just recognised the need for brandy as a preservative agent in the days before fridges. A very sweet old lady – this was her mother's recipe.

THE KEY: The planning. You need to know when you'll have time to bake the cake so you can start soaking the fruit a week in advance. Don't skimp on this – a week it says, so a week it must be.

Note
When you remove it from the tin, leave the lining paper intact. Refrigerate in plastic clingfilm for up to 1 year.

Degree of Difficulty: 3   **Serves** 14–16

Ingredients

250 g each chopped sultanas, raisins, dates

125 g each currants, mixed peel, glacé cherries, glacé apricots

½ cup brandy

250 g butter

1 cup brown sugar, well packed

5 eggs

½ cup standard flour

⅓ cup self-raising flour

½ teaspoon mixed spice

Oven temp: 150°C

Method

1. Preheat the oven to 150°C.
2. Mix the dried fruit and brandy, cover and leave to soak for 1 week.
3. Cream the butter and sugar.
4. Add the eggs, one at a time, beating well after each addition.
5. Add the mixture to the boozy fruit and mix well.
6. Sift the dry ingredients and stir them in, mixing well.
7. Spoon the mixture into a triple-lined 23 cm cake tin. Triple-lined means 3 layers of baking paper in the bottom of the tin, cut into a circular shape to match the base. Then grease the sides of the tin with butter and use a strip of baking paper the same height as the tin and line all the way around the sides. The butter will help the baking paper stick to the tin.
8. Bake for about 3–3½ hours.
9. When cooked, brush with extra brandy while it's still warm.

ORANGE CHOCOLATE LOAF

REMEMBER Steve Austin? Sure, that seems a random question, but stick with me and you'll see where I'm going.

Steve Austin was a pretty cool guy before the bionics. He was an astronaut! And you just know he had a way with the ladies. But after the crash Oscar took Steve and made him even better. Better, stronger, faster.

And that's what happened to this loaf. It was a pretty good citrus loaf to begin with. And then I had this idea that, to be honest, I nicked from somewhere else. I wondered if the loaf would be even better if I added some chocolate and zest and just marbled it through, rather than mixing it. And it was. Better, stronger, faster (cue theme music).

THE KEY: Follow the order of ingredients. Adding the milk and OJ together will be like telling your wife you're off to the footy on her birthday – you'll get an unfavourable reaction.

Suggestion

- *As you've done with the lemon madeira, just squeeze orange juice over the top of the loaf and sprinkle it with sugar instead of killing the thing with heavy icing.*

Degree of Difficulty: 3   **Makes** 1 loaf

Ingredients

zest of 1 orange
½ cup grated dark chocolate
125 g butter, softened
¾ cup sugar
2 eggs, whisked
juice of 1 single orange
1½ cups standard flour
1½ teaspoons baking powder
½ cup milk

Oven temp: 190°C

Method

1. Preheat the oven to 190°C.
2. Combine the orange zest and chocolate and set aside.
3. Cream the softened butter and sugar together.
4. Add the whisked eggs and beat well for 1 minute. Add the juice.
5. Fold in the sifted flour and baking powder.
6. Add the milk last.
7. Pour half the cake mix into a greased 20 cm loaf tin.
8. Scatter half the chocolate/orange zest mix over that, then tip the rest of the cake mix in and top it off with the remainder of the choc/zest.
9. Pull a knife through the lot a couple of times to get a marbled effect.
10. Bake for about 45 minutes.

FRANCIE'S CARROT CAKE
(Francie Brierly)

ON THE WEST COAST of the North Island is a small town famous for its surf and long, black sand beaches. It's packed with boutique shops and top notch nosh stops. Yep, it's Raglan.

Francie owns and runs a place there called 'Pearl Elliot', which folk can rent. There are too many things to recommend this heavenly hideaway to list here. But leading the way would be the home baking. Francie not only left us the most delicious carrot cake but she let me have the recipe, too.

 THE KEY: Brown sugar, according to Francie, is the secret to all baking. She never uses any other kind.

Suggestion

- *Great with cream cheese icing (see page 164) or for something different try tangy butter icing (page 162).*

Degree of Difficulty: 3　　　　　　**Serves** 10

Ingredients

260 ml canola oil

330 g brown sugar

4 eggs

3 cups grated carrots

100 g currants

100 g sultanas

½ cup walnuts, crunched in your hands to break them up

165 g standard flour

40 g cornflour

1 heaped teaspoon baking soda

1 teaspoon each ginger, cinnamon, mixed spice

Oven temp:
150°C

Method

1. Preheat the oven to 150°C.
2. Line a 24 cm cake tin with greased baking paper.
3. Cream the oil and brown sugar and add the eggs. Whisk well.
4. Add the carrots, currants, sultanas and nuts.
5. Stir in the dry ingredients.
6. Bake for about 1 hour or until a skewer inserted into the middle of the cake comes out clean.

COCONUT CAKE WITH LIGHT LEMON ICING

A FEW YEARS AGO the boss shouted the whole team a trip to Fiji. That kind of thing doesn't happen any more – nothing to do with the recession, he was just unhappy about all the inappropriate carrying on. Ah, those were the days.

The place we stayed had one of those pools with a bar in it. You could swim right up to the stool, sit down and order your Malibu and lemonade, then carry on carrying on inappropriately without even having to dry off. Long story short: I've come up with an alcohol-free way to capture that relaxed, poolside feeling without having to pay for a trip to the islands.

THE KEY: Desiccated coconut. If you only have shredded in the pantry then that'll do, but the texture of the cake is about 100 times better if the coconut is really fine.

Suggestions

- *As I said at the start, this goes perfectly with a light lemon icing (see page 160) and add a touch more water. Just a touch though – you don't want it to be runny.*
- *A nice alternative if that doesn't float your boat is to top the cake with tangy butter icing. Really sweet and delicious.*

Degree of Difficulty: 2   **Serves** 8

Ingredients

1 cup brown sugar, well packed

125 g butter

1 teaspoon vanilla essence

1½ cups standard flour

2 teaspoons baking powder

1 cup desiccated coconut

3 eggs, whisked

½ cup milk

Oven temp: 160°C

Method

1. Preheat the oven to 160°C.
2. Grease or line a 20 cm round cake tin.
3. Combine the sugar, butter and vanilla in a pot over a low heat and give it a good stir.
4. Once it's nice and smooth, take it off the heat and sift in the flour and baking powder.
5. Stir in the coconut and mix it through.
6. Chuck in the whisked eggs and milk and give the batter a whisk for a minute or so.
7. Tip it into the prepped tin.
8. Bake for about for 45–50 minutes.

SPICY CINNAMON CAKE

MY WIFE called and said she was bringing a friend home for dinner. Would I make a cake for dessert? They'd be home in an hour.

An hour to make a cake? I could've said no, of course. To my wife. Of course.

Anyway, I had this recipe that a bloke I know had given me. I'd already had a look at it and made a few minor modifications and I figured it would be the most likely one to come in on time and under budget. Whaddya know, it worked out perfect.

Timing. Give the cake the tap test at 20 minutes. That is: gently press the middle of it with one finger (doesn't matter which one). If it springs back in the middle it's done. If not, try again at 25. If you reckon it's nearly there pull it out, cover with tinfoil and let it finish cooking outside the oven.

 There's a risk of dryness if it goes full term.

Suggestions

- *You can just dust it with icing sugar and serve as is. Or serve it warm with vanilla ice cream and maple syrup.*
- *If you've got the time and inclination, melt 2 tablespoons of golden syrup with 1 teaspoon of butter. Whip about 150–200 ml of cream, then fold the syrup through the cream and serve a spoonful on the side with the cake.*

Degree of Difficulty: 2   **Serves** 8

Ingredients

125 g butter

⅔ cup sugar

2 eggs

1 cup standard flour

2 teaspoons baking powder

2 teaspoons cinnamon

1 teaspoon ground ginger

1 teaspoon mixed spice

Oven temp: 180°C

Method

1. Preheat the oven to 180°C.
2. Cream the butter and sugar until light and smooth.
3. In a separate bowl beat or whisk the eggs until really frothy. Add the result to the butter and sugar and keep on whisking until it gets to a stage you'd call 'creamy'.
4. Sift in the flour, baking powder and spices and fold them through.
5. Tip it all into a greased 20 cm cake tin.
6. Bake for about 25 minutes.

THE WORLD'S EASIEST FRUIT CAKE

THIS RECIPE was given to me by a bloke named Barry, which leads me to issue the following two separate challenges.

Challenge 1: Try and come up with a blokier name than Barry. I know some good blokes named Wayne, but the name itself doesn't meet the challenge. Chuck, Chip and Charlie are out. Bruce would go close. Barry might just be the blokiest name there is.

Challenge 2: Try and find an easier fruit cake recipe. Or don't bother. Because – and I don't want to cast doubts over your ability – you won't.

THE KEY: Soaking. It's got to be overnight. Don't come home from work and think you can start soaking to make the cake that evening. Overnight, minimum.

Degree of Difficulty: 2   **Serves** 8–10

Ingredients

1 kg fruit mix
2 cups strong black coffee
2 cups self-raising flour
1 teaspoon mixed spice

Oven temp: 180°C

Method

1. Preheat the oven to 180°C.
2. Soak the fruit mix overnight in the coffee.
3. Sift in the flour, add the spice and mix it all together.
4. Tip into a lined 20 cm cake tin.
5. Bake for about 1 hour 20–1 hour 30 minutes.

YOGHURT CAKE

OURS IS A YOGHURT FAMILY. The wife has her fancy fig and petunia yoghurt, our son is a fan of whichever flavour has the Wiggles on it this week and I'll grab the yoghurt that's on special. As you can imagine, with all that yoghurt in one fridge there is, every now and then, some left over.

And when this happens, I make this super-quick, incredibly easy and delicious recipe. In my book that combination is worth three big tasty stars.

Here's how to make it even easier — grab a 150 ml pot of yoghurt and empty it into a bowl. Then rinse it and use it to measure the other ingredients.

Degree of Difficulty: 2   **Serves** 8

Ingredients

175 g butter, softened, not melted

2 pots sugar

2 eggs

1 x 150 ml pot yoghurt, any flavour

3 pots standard flour

3 teaspoons baking powder

Oven temp: 160°C

Method

1. Preheat the oven to 160°C.
2. Grease a 21–23 cm cake tin.
3. Cream the butter and sugar.
4. Add the eggs, one at a time, and whisk well after each one.
5. Chuck in the yoghurt and keep whisking.
6. Sift in the flour and baking powder and mix it through.
7. Bake for about 50–60 minutes.

Pies, Quiches *and* Savouries

Understanding the Lingo

Season. (v) pron: SEE-zin

a) *The part of the year during which a particular sport is played.*

b) *A specific period with a given start and finish date during which hunting of a specific animal, fish or bird is allowed.*

c) *Grabbin' from someone else (such as 'control').*

IN THE WORLD OF SAVOURY cooking or baking one of the most important things you can know how to do is season. This essentially means the appropriate use of salt and pepper. Most people will under-season in the fear that the person eating the dish won't appreciate too much of either. That's a mistake. The key to seasoning is taste-testing. In fact, that's the key to getting the flavour right at any time. Use a clean teaspoon and as you cook the pie filling (or whatever it is you're making) try it as you go.

Be careful, though, with taste-testing uncooked fillings such as raw egg. If it's quiche you're making always just follow the guidelines of the recipe.

'Who ate all the pies?
Who ate all the pies?'

Traditional sports chant, sung to the tune of 'Knees Up Mother Brown', usually aimed at overweight opposing players or supporters.

SAVOURY SHORTCRUST PASTRY

SOME PEOPLE think making pastry is difficult, but it's actually not – and even though a lot of blokes can bake a reasonable cake or turn out a batch of pretty good muffins, not many seem willing to give pastry a crack. And the odd thing about this fact is that making pastry is, ironically, a piece of cake. On top of which home-made pastry tastes 10 times better than any of the stuff you can buy.

Make a heap of it and freeze what you don't need (unbaked pastry will last up to about 8 weeks in the freezer). This recipe is good for a couple of decent tarts or pies (using a 20–21 cm dish) so you could make one now and another in a few weeks.

So here we go – I'm starting the pie chapter the same way I started the tart chapter: here's the best, most useful shortcrust pastry you'll ever need.

THE KEY: At the risk of repeating myself, there are two important parts to this process. When squeezing the flour through the butter, keep going until it's really evenly mixed. Then, when pressing it out before chilling it, make sure you turn or fold and knead no more than four times.

TOP TIP

When kneading the pastry before chilling it, form it into a round shape (like a thick pancake), which will make it much easier to roll afterwards.

Degree of Difficulty: 2
This makes enough for two bases in a 20–21 cm shallow pie dish, or one pie in a deep dish (including the pie top).

Ingredients

2 cups standard flour
pinch of salt
120 g butter, chilled
1 egg
2 tablespoons lemon juice

Method

1. Sift the flour into a bowl with the salt.
2. Grate in the chilled butter.
3. Smoosh it all together with a fork, then get your fingers in and squeeze the butter through the flour until it looks like breadcrumbs.
4. Use a spoon to make a well in the centre and crack in the egg. Working from the centre, mix it in with a fork, then squeeze in the lemon juice. Slowly add a little water and start working the mixture together with your hands.
5. As soon as it's a 'rollable' consistency, knead it a couple of times, but not too much.
6. Wrap the dough in plastic clingfilm and chuck it in the fridge for at least 30 minutes.

Note

Read up about baking blind (see page 114) so, depending on what you want to use the pastry for, you'll have it under control.

BEER BREAD

A FEW YEARS BACK I was invited to appear on a kids' TV show, which involved getting there a bit early to get my make-up done. I'll be honest – I was more concerned about people thinking I had make-up on than anything else. But when I walked into the make-up room, who should be sitting there having powder applied to his mug but All Black hard man Richard Loe – he of the nose-breaking forearm and menacing glare.

These days I do the occasional bit of baking on the goggle box and every time I step into the make-up room I still think of Richard Loe sitting in that chair – his kauri-like forearms resting at his side while a lovely lady named Liz dabbed foundation under his eyes.

None of which has much to do with anything, except that of all the things I've baked on TV this recipe has received far and away the biggest, most favourable response. It's just about the easiest thing you'll ever make and it turns out great every time.

 THE KEY: Don't forget the salt.

Suggestions

- *Peter A has tried this loaf with various beers and has yet to come across one that doesn't work. Pale ale, stout, it's all fine.*
- *Our mate Brett reckons adding 2 teaspoons of cajun spices (a premixed combination that you can buy at the supermarket) works well, too.*
- *Experiment with some extra ingredients. As long as you stay with the base elements and the ratios there's not much that can go wrong.*

Degree of Difficulty: 2   **Makes** 1 loaf

Ingredients

1½ cups standard flour

1½ cups wholemeal flour

3 teaspoons baking powder

1 teaspoon salt

1 x 400 ml can or bottle full-strength beer

½ cup grated cheese

Oven temp: 200°C

Method

1. Preheat the oven to 200°C.
2. Mix together the dry ingredients, then add the beer. If it's a bit dry mix in a little extra liquid. Mix well.
3. Tip into a well-greased loaf tin and sprinkle the cheese on the top.
4. Bake for 50–60 minutes.

Note

Being a sharp-eyed bloke you probably noted that cans or stubbies usually hold less than 400 ml. To make up the liquid I add a warm water/oil mix of about 50 ml water and 20 ml vegetable oil.

CHEESE AND BACON MINI MUFFINS

IN THE BACK of your pots and pans cupboard, deep in the area reserved for tins and moulds that you never use, there'll probably be a mini-muffin tray. It's likely that it's been sitting there since you last had cause to make mini-muffins in the late 1970s.

You could, of course, use this recipe to make standard-sized muffins, but trust me. If you're going to a poker night, or to a mate's place to watch rugby, these are just the right size to stuff in your gob between swigs of your favourite amber liquid. You can also use them to buy back into the game after you try and bluff with an 'all-in' call on a pair of threes and lose everything. At least, that's what I did.

 Put some elbow grease into the whisking. Get that egg looking like a good head of beer.

Suggestion

- *Instead of bacon, use 100 g of hot-smoked salmon. Use a fork to shred the salmon and mix as above. They're even better this way, but less blokey.*

Degree of Difficulty: 2   **Makes** 24 little muffins

Ingredients

1 cup standard flour

3 teaspoons baking powder

1 egg

½ cup milk

1 cup grated cheese (tasty)

1 cup chopped bacon

Oven temp:
200°C

Method

1. Preheat the oven to 200°C.
2. Sift the flour and baking powder into a bowl.
3. In a separate bowl whisk the egg until it's frothy.
4. Tip the egg, milk, cheese and bacon into the flour and mix.
5. Done. Just like that.
6. Bake for about 10 minutes.

Note

If you don't have a mini-muffin tray, you can do these as a kind of savoury rock-cake. Grease a piece of baking paper and line your baking tray. Put big teaspoonsful of the mix onto the tray. You'll end up with about 24.

BACON AND EGG PIE

MY MATE STU nicked this recipe and modified it a little before handing it over to me. I like Stu and I won't hear a bad word said about him, but let's be honest – this pie is probably the best thing he's ever done (outside of fathering a couple of pretty good kids).

It doesn't get much simpler or blokier than bacon and eggs wrapped in buttery pastry. Every now and then, over a cold one across the road, Stu will get all misty eyed, look off into the distance and sigh. Then he'll say something like, 'Mate – that's a hell of a pie.' And he's right.

THE KEY: Lazy blokes might want to buy pastry, but it's just as quick and easy to make your own and it makes all the difference to the end product (see page 94).

REVIEWS

Ray: *Bacon bits are cheaper than rashers and already chopped.*
Kerry: *Great stuff. I added two cooked portions of spinach and half a block of feta cheese.*
Tonka: *Tastes choice.*
Rhozie: *Even better with finely chopped red onion and parsley.*

Degree of Difficulty: 3   **Serves** 6 – 8

Ingredients

savoury shortcrust pastry (see page 94 –
   you need everything that recipe makes)
1 cup grated cheese
500–750 g bacon (best to use good rashers
   chopped into bits with the rind cut off)
7–9 eggs
salt and pepper
milk or beaten egg to glaze

Oven temp: 200°C

Method

1. Preheat the oven to 200°C.
2. Press most of the pastry into the bottom of a greased 24 cm deep-dish pie tin (don't press too hard!).
3. Sprinkle the grated cheese over the pastry followed by the bacon pieces.
4. Break in the eggs (not including the shell) and then jab the yolks with a fork so they spread.
5. Add more bacon and more egg until you're happy.
6. Use the rest of the pastry to make a top – jab holes in it with a fork and glaze with a little milk or beaten egg.
7. Bake for 20–30 minutes.

SMOKED TUNA BREAD CASES
(Jeff Cameron)

JEFF GOT THIS RECIPE from his grandmother. During World War 2 there was rationing in place and many groceries were hard to get. His grandfather used to help by catching fish and smoking it right there on the shore on sticks over a fire with manuka sawdust.

Grandma baked her own bread and when it got a little stale she would brush it with milk from their house cow and make smoked fish bread cases. She could make a little go a long way. She had to: Jeff has two aunties and five uncles so there were 10 people in the house.

She made them for Jeff and his brother when they were little and stayed with them on their remote bush farm out the back of Waverly in south Taranaki. He got the recipe years later along with a couple of others just before she died at the age of 83. Cheers, Grandma!

THE KEY: Make a double batch of the cheese sauce. Also, cool the cases on a wire rack because if you try and scoff 'em while they're hot they fall apart.

Suggestion

- *This is perfect for filling up the boys when they come around to bludge off your Sky subscription by watching the game at your place.*

Degree of Difficulty: 3   **Makes** 12

Ingredients
cheese sauce (see page 170)
1 x 185 g can smoked tuna
1 loaf white sandwich bread
parsley
salt and pepper

Oven temp: 180°C

Method
1. Preheat the oven to 180°C.
2. Make up a double batch of the cheese sauce on page 170 and whisk in some chopped parsley. OK – that's the hardest part done.
3. Drain the tuna and add it to the cheese sauce. Set aside.
4. Cut the crusts off the bread, then butter each slice on one side. Press the slices into a 12-cup muffin tray, butter side down, so they stick to the sides.
5. Spoon the white sauce/tuna mix into the bread cases.
6. Bake for 20 minutes or until the edges of the bread go brown.
7. Remove them from the muffin tray and cool on a wire rack (be careful – they need to cool down before you get stuck in – otherwise they'll fall apart).

BIG FISH PIE

A COUPLE OF YEARS AGO I was further north visiting my folks. It so happened that while I was staying there was a big local fishing contest. I'm hopeless with a rod. The number of fish I've caught in my whole life would be countable on the left hand of an unlucky carpenter.

My Mum, however, is fantastic. She's been keen on fishing all her life, and especially ocean fishing. So when the contest was done, and the catch had been weighed (hers was a flippin' great big snapper), she was proud as punch to come third in the ladies section after which there was a prize-giving at the club and she was awarded a trophy.

As if that wasn't enough, my little brother Tony won both the raffles that same evening. How about that for a lucky run?

We used the snapper to make this pie.

 THE KEY: Halfway through the baking (at about 20 minutes) lay a sheet of tinfoil across the top so the pie cooks, but the pastry doesn't burn.

Suggestions

- *This is also good made with tuna or – if your budget is huge – try smoked salmon (in which case skip the precooking step).*
- *If you have extra pastry from lining the tin and trimming the top layer, make shapes and stick them on top.*

Degree of Difficulty: 4   **Serves** 8–10

Ingredients

900 g –1 kg fish fillets (snapper is good, but your choice)

oil for cooking

1 onion, peeled and chopped

8 leeks, chopped chunky style

200 ml cream

3 egg yolks

salt and pepper

savoury shortcrust pastry (see page 94)

Oven temp: 180°C

Method

1. Preheat the oven to 180°C.
2. Steam the fish for 8 minutes or zap it in the microwave for about 2 minutes to partially cook it.
3. Put a little oil in a frying pan and over a low heat stir-fry the onion and leeks together for a few minutes.
4. Drain off the excess moisture in a sieve.
5. Chop up the fish and chuck it in a bowl. Tip in the onion/leek mixture, the cream and 2 of the egg yolks and mix thoroughly. Season to taste.
6. Prep a deep pie dish – or a 24 cm cake tin – by greasing it.
7. Line the dish with most of the pastry (hold some back for the top).
8. Fill about three-quarters of the way to the top with the mixture.
9. Roll out the remaining pastry and lay on top, brush butter around the edge, then fold the sides down and press gently to create a kind of border all the way around.
10. Lightly whisk the remaining egg yolk and use it to brush the top and edges of the pastry.
11. Bake for about 40 minutes.

QUICHE LARRY

GENTLEMEN AND BLOKES, I give you the European way of making bacon and egg pie.

This recipe started out in a region in France called Loraine, which is why it's usually called Quiche Loraine. The standard Loraine has chopped-up chunks of bacon and Swiss cheese in it. In my very blokey version of the same thing you ditch the Swiss (who've ruined the America's Cup anyway) and include a smattering of good old-fashioned cheddar. Hence the sex-change (in that Loraine becomes Larry). Enjoy.

 THE KEY: Good quality bacon. There's a great range available out there but if you've got a good butcher then that'd be the place to start.

TOP TIP

For best results stick the pastry back into the fridge for 30 minutes once you've pressed it into the dish. This will help stop it from dropping and shrinking.

Degree of Difficulty: 3   **Serves** 6–8

Ingredients

savoury shortcrust pastry (see page 94. You'll need about
  half of what that recipe makes. Freeze the rest)
2 eggs
250 ml cream
salt and pepper
400 g bacon bits
  (chopped up rashers with the rind removed)
½ cup grated tasty cheese

Oven temp:
200°C

Method

1. Preheat the oven to 200°C.
2. Prep a 23 cm pie or tart dish by greasing the inside of it with butter.
3. On a lightly floured surface roll out the pastry to the same size as the pie dish (allowing enough for the sides). Line the bottom and sides of the dish with the pastry and press it gently into the dish. Jab evenly around the base with a fork a dozen or so times.
4. Bake blind for 10 minutes (see page 114).
5. While that's happening, whisk together the eggs, cream, salt and pepper until they're nice and smooth.
6. Spread the chopped bacon bits around the base of the pie.
7. Chuck the grated cheese over the top of the bacon.
8. Pour the eggy mixture over the top and stick the lot in the oven.
9. Bake for 20 minutes.

SALMON AND BROCCOLI QUICHE

WHILE WE'RE ON THE SUBJECT OF QUICHE, here's another one for you to try.

For a bloke's book this one doesn't sound very blokey, but that's because you're thinking of fancy pink salmon. Surprisingly, salmon could well be the blokiest of all the fish species. These extremely manly fish set off from their happy abodes in the ocean, working against the current, with the intention of finishing upstream, a distance that can be thousands of miles. On the way they fight off predators, undergo a physical change because they've moved into fresh water and occasionally get caught and eaten by the likes of us.

And why do they do this? One reason only: to impress chicks.

Seriously, when was the last time you did something that blokey? Salmon has a well-deserved place in this book. I've partnered it here with broccoli because it is, in the vegetable world, just about the best source of iron (very blokey). But if you're still not convinced, think of it as 'man-fish and iron pie'.

THE KEY: Use the right kind of smoked salmon. You don't want the slivers of cold-smoked stuff; you want a chunk of wood-roasted salmon (available in the fish section of the supermarket) that comes pre-packed in 100 or 200 g packets.

TOP TIP

As with any other pie or tart, it'll help avoid sagging or drooping pastry if you put the pastry back into the fridge once you've pressed it into the dish.

Degree of Difficulty: 3 **Serves** 6–8

Ingredients

savoury shortcrust pastry (see page 94. You need about half
   of what the recipe makes.)
2 eggs
250 ml cream
½ teaspoon nutmeg
salt and pepper
200 g uncooked broccoli, chopped into small pieces
200 g smoked salmon, shredded with a fork

Oven temp:
200°C

Method

1. Preheat the oven to 200°C.
2. Prep a 23 cm pie dish by greasing the inside of it with butter.
3. Lightly flour the bench and roll out the pastry to the same size as the pie dish (allowing enough for the sides). Line the bottom and sides of the dish with the pastry, pressing it gently into the dish. Jab evenly around the base with a fork a dozen or so times.
4. Bake blind for 10 minutes (see page 114).
5. While that's happening, whisk together the eggs and cream, nutmeg, salt and pepper until they're nice and smooth.
6. Spread the chopped broccoli and shredded salmon around the base of the pie.
7. Pour the eggy mixture over the top and stick the lot in the oven.
8. Bake for 20 minutes.

EASY MEAT PIE
(Brad)

WHEN I WAS JUST A NIPPER at a brand-new school I was caught offguard one day and made a terrible, life-changing admission to the wrong person.

The scene was music class. I was 12 years old. The kid I was talking to, whose name I honestly don't remember, was asking about this and that in a friendly, interested way and snuck a question in about my favourite band. And just like that, without thinking, I told him that it was ABBA.

This was about five years after everyone had stopped liking ABBA and as soon as I said it he howled with laughter, called out for everyone else's attention and then shouted to the class what I'd said. Pretty soon everyone else was laughing and that lunchtime I was given a butt-kicking. The connection to this particular recipe is that on that day I was the easy meat.

 THE KEY: The mashed spud and the stock, which gives the pie body and flavour – so don't skip these important ingredients.

Note
While pork and beef is a good combination, you can use just one or the other if you prefer.

Degree of Difficulty: 4   **Serves** 8

Ingredients

2 sheets savoury shortcrust pastry (or see the recipe on page 94)

1 tablespoon butter

1 large onion, peeled and sliced

450 g beef mince

450 g pork mince

1 cup mashed potato

1 chicken stock cube, crushed

salt and pepper to season

½ cup grated cheese

Oven temp: 190°C

Method

1. Preheat the oven to 190°C.
2. Grease a 21 cm deep-dish pie tin.
3. Line the bottom and sides of the dish with 1 sheet of the pastry, pressing it gently into the dish.
4. Bake blind for about 10 minutes (see page 114).
5. While that's happening, heat the butter in a frying pan and cook the onion until it's lightly golden, then put it to one side.
6. In a large pot brown the beef and pork mince in a little oil.
7. When it's no longer pink, add the mashed potato, the cooked onion and the crushed stock cube.
8. Season with salt and pepper.
9. Mix well and then spoon into the pie base.
10. Roll out the second sheet of pastry and use to cover the filling.
11. Poke holes in the top to let the steam escape and bake for 25 minutes.
12. Remove from the oven, scatter the top with the grated cheese and bake for a further 10 minutes.

BACON AND CAPSICUM MUFFINS

THERE ARE SOME THINGS in the world that sit just outside easy categorisation. They look like one thing, but are officially another. A good example of this is Cher. Other examples include:

- Darts and poker: as sedate as they seem, both are sports (they are, after all, on the sports channel).
- Boy George: enough said.
- Peanuts: not a nut at all, but a legume.
- Crayfish: not a fish, despite the name. It is, in fact, a crustacean.

Which brings me to capsicum. Also known as red pepper, it is not a vegetable. Like cucumber, tomato and pumpkin, it has seeds and is therefore a fruit. I do not, however, want it in my fruit salad.

THE KEY: Buy good quality ingredients. The pre-packed bacon bits from the supermarket are cheaper and more convenient, but they don't taste a patch on really good bacon. It makes all the difference.

Suggestion

- *If you want to go to just a little more trouble, char-grill the capsicum before chopping it up. It changes the flavour – in a very good way. Of course, I understand that you might not think it worth the trouble, but I reckon you'll like it.*

Degree of Difficulty: 3

Makes 12 regular muffins or about 24 small ones.

¼ cup cooking oil

1 egg, whisked

1 cup milk

½ cup cooked, chopped bacon, cooled

2 cups standard flour

pinch of salt

4 teaspoons baking powder

½ red capsicum, deseeded and chopped

1 cup grated tasty cheese

pepper to taste (optional)

Oven temp:
200°C

1. Preheat the oven to 200°C.
2. Tip the oil into the whisked egg and mix well. Get it nice and frothy and then add the milk.
3. Add the cooled bacon and give the mixture a stir.
4. Sift in the flour, salt and baking powder, then fold it all together.
5. As you're folding, add the capsicum and cheese. You could grind in a little pepper here, too.
6. Spoon the mix into a well-greased muffin tray (you can use a mini-muffin tray or standard 12 cup tray).
7. Bake for about 25 minutes.

Desserts, Tarts *and* Treats

Understanding the Lingo

Bake Blind. (v) pron: Bay-k Blyn-d

a) *To have too many drinks before you start baking (not considered a very good idea by most).*

b) *To wear a piece of cloth over your eyes while you bake (see def. 1 for note on this as a bad idea, even if you have been dared by friends after having too many drinks).*

c) *A Venetian blind that is installed so that it can be closed when the home owner is baking.*

A LOT OF BLOKES are unduly worried about baking blind. It simply means that you need to bake the pastry by itself for a while, without the filling or topping. When you have to do it just follow these steps:

- Press your pastry gently into the tin, tray or dish that you're using.
- Stick a piece of baking paper over the top of the pastry and use your fingers to carefully shape it to the pastry.
- Pour rice on top of the baking paper so that it becomes the stand-in pie filling (you can buy specially made beads or small ceramic stones for baking blind but I find rice just as good and a lot cheaper).
- Bake it for the time called for in the recipe.

That's it!

❛ If you don't eat your meat you can't have any pudding. ❜

Brick in the Wall album, Pink Floyd

❛ Let us celebrate with the adding of chocolate! ❜

– Homer Simpson

SWEET SHORTCRUST PASTRY

HERE ARE TWO GAMES worth playing. One of them might even win you some cash.

When my brothers and I were all still in our teens I watched with interest when my brother, David, told our youngest brother, Tony, that he'd give him $50 if Tony would let him smash two raw eggs over his head. Tony said, 'Fifty?' David said, 'Two eggs for fifty bucks. Five-Oh.' 'Sure,' said Tony.

David smashed one egg on top of Tony's head and rubbed the yolk in nice and hard. Then he walked away. 'I changed my mind,' he said. 'I don't feel like doing the second egg.' He kept his fifty and even Tony had to see the funny side of it . . . after a while.

In the second game my friend Stu bet me $10 that he could make shortcrust pastry faster than I could get to the dairy, buy some and return again. I took that bet. What Stu didn't know was that the dairy is literally just around the corner. What I didn't know was that they didn't stock shortcrust pastry. I had to jump in the car and go to the supermarket. Needless to say Stu won the bet.

Which reminds me – I still owe him a tenner.

THE KEY: There are two important parts to this process. First, when you're squeezing the flour through the butter, keep going until it's really evenly mixed. Second, when pressing it out, before you stick it in the fridge to chill, make sure you turn or fold and knead no more than four times.

TOP TIP

When you start kneading the pastry, form it into a round shape about the size of a thick saucer. This makes it easier to roll out afterwards when you're ready to turn it into a pie or whatever.

Degree of Difficulty: *2*

This makes enough pastry for two bases in a 20–21cm tart tin.

Ingredients

2 cups standard flour
pinch of salt
2 tablespoons icing sugar
120 g butter, chilled
1 egg
2 tablespoons lemon juice
water

Method

1. Sift the flour into a bowl with the salt, and then mix through the icing sugar.
2. Grate the butter into the bowl.
3. Smoosh it all together with a fork, then get your fingers in and squeeze the butter through the flour until it goes like breadcrumbs.
4. Make a well in the centre with a spoon and crack in the egg. Mix in the egg working from the centre then squeeze in the lemon juice. Slowly add a little water and start working the mixture together with your hands.
5. As soon as it's of a 'rollable' consistency, turn it out onto a lightly floured bench and knead it a couple of times – but not too much.
6. Wrap the dough in plastic clingfilm and chuck it in the fridge for at least 30 minutes.

Note

Bone up on the art of baking blind (see page 114). You really need to know what this is all about if you're serious about making your own pastry.

SWEET BERRY PIZZA

SOME PEOPLE are natural tossers, and while it's tempting to think I might be one of them, it turns out I'm not.

A while back I was asked to judge a pizza-tossing contest. Really all the folks had to do was roll out a pizza base and then hurl it into the air. The best tossers had the thing spinning up and away like a Frisbee and then returning to their flattened hand so they could send it skyward again. Before the contest started the organisers thought it would be good if I could demonstrate. Which I tried to do. I rolled and floured and threw. My pizza base went straight up, hit the ceiling and then came down fast, catching on my thumb. We had to throw that one away because of the big hole and the funny shape.

Not much of a tosser, me, which is why these pizzas are just rolled out shortcrust pastry. Much easier.

THE KEY: The right-sized tools. Whatever size you're cutting your pizza to, you need a slightly smaller flat-bottom plate to sit on it while it blind bakes.

Note

There's no need to weight the ramekin or bowl sitting on the pastry with rice or pasta. The weight of the dish itself should do the trick.

Degree of Difficulty: 2   **Makes** 4 to 6 mini pizzas

Ingredients

2 sheets shortcrust pastry
  (bought or make your own, see page 94)
2–3 punnets fresh berries
  (I like a strawberry/blueberry combo.)
250 ml crème pâtissière (see page 168)

Oven temp:
200°C

Method

1. Preheat the oven to 200°C.
2. Using an upside-down dessert bowl as your cookie cutter, cut out four rounds of pastry and place them on a greased baking tray.
3. Sit a slightly smaller flat-bottomed ovenproof bowl or plate on top of each pastry round so that about 1 cm of pastry is exposed all the way around. The idea is that the pastry will rise slightly at the edges and remain flat in the centre.
4. Blind bake the pastry for 15 minutes or until the edges are golden.
5. Allow to cool, then assemble by spreading crème pâtissière on the base and topping with fresh berries.

SCROGGIN
(Jeff Cameron)

MY MATE JEFF told me about the time he was hunting with the old man around Little River on Stewart Island quite a few years ago and bumped into a Swedish tourist who was tenting just up off the beach. The guy offered them some stuff that he said was Scroggin.

Jeff reckons he's never eaten anything as nice as this stuff, and he's never struck it again, so 32 years later he had a go. In his version the trail mix is mixed through uncooked biscuit dough. The main thing is the dough can't have raw egg in it or you could get crook guts. He had salmonella once, he tells me – not good!

 THE KEY: When you get to mixing in the trail mix, just put in enough to suit your taste. Don't go too nuts (ha!) though, or it'll fall apart.

Suggestion

- *This is great as an at-school or after-school snack for the kids. In fact, forget the kids, it's just the thing to take to work as an energy booster during the day when working with turkeys starts to become draining.*

Degree of Difficulty: 2   **Makes** 3–4 cups

Ingredients

3 tablespoons brown sugar

3 tablespoons white sugar

2 tablespoons butter, softened but not melted

½ teaspoon vanilla essence

2 tablespoons milk or water

½ cup standard flour

2–3 cups trail mix, i.e. a mixture of chocolate chips, dried fruit and nuts

Method

1. Stick all the sugar and the butter in a bowl and cream until smooth.
2. Stir in the vanilla and milk or water.
3. Sift in the flour and mix until well blended.
4. Add in the trail mix and stir through.
5. Once it's nice and chunky, tip into a plastic container and away you go.

BREAD PUDDING

REMEMBER BACK when we didn't wear bike helmets and played bull-rush? There was milk bottle delivery right to your house but only two TV channels, neither of which went later than 10 or 11 pm. Those were the days of the Goodnight Kiwi, getting the strap at school and blowing the dust off the needle before you put it down on the record. Going to the movies was a big deal and it only cost a couple of bucks, for which you'd get a cartoon and intermission as well as the feature.

Bread pudding is a throwback to those days – before the advent of Playstations and websites and ipods and cellphones and palm pilots and downloading and TiVo and cyber-bullying. Unlike most of our misty-eyed memories, though, this one stands up today. The first bite is likely to bring a nostalgic twitching to the lips that might almost be a smile.

 THE KEY: Don't dodge the 30-minute chill. Let your bread soak up the custard before you get the heat cranked up.

Suggestions

- *Cut the bread into any shape you want, e.g. triangles look good. But if you're going to do that, why not just cut out heart shapes and be done with it.*
- *I use leftover French bread (after the wife's bought a couple of sticks for a swanky do, but only uses half of one of them). Or, and this is less regular, if you can talk your local bakery into unloading half a dozen of yesterday's croissants, they make a cracker bread pudding. Slice them in half and layer as you'd do with bread slices.*

Degree of Difficulty: 2   **Serves** 8

Ingredients

6–8 slices white bread, cut into squares, crusts off

½ cup sultanas or raisins

3 eggs

¼ cup sugar

1 cup milk

1 cup cream

½ teaspoon vanilla essence

½ teaspoon cinnamon

icing sugar for dusting

Oven temp:
180°C

Method

1. Preheat the oven to 180°C.
2. Arrange the bread squares in an ovenproof dish so they're overlapping.
3. Sprinkle the sultanas or raisins evenly over the top.
4. In a bowl whisk together the eggs and sugar.
5. In a separate bowl, mix together the milk, cream and vanilla.
6. Slowly add the milky mixture to the sugar and eggs to make a runny custard. Stir in the cinnamon.
7. Pour the custard over the bread. It should look like the bread is in a milky bath right up to its neck.
8. Cover and chill for at least 30 minutes but preferably 1 hour.
9. Bake for about 30 minutes.
10. Once baked, dust with icing sugar before serving. I think it's a lot better served warm.

CHOCOLATE BREAD PUDDING

GREAT combinations:
- Batman and Robin
- Laurel and Hardy
- Cheech and Chong
- The Lone Ranger and Tonto
- Starsky and Hutch/Bodie and Doyle
- Fish and chips
- And this: bread pudding and chocolate.

I nabbed this recipe from a magazine that had gone a little crazy on the fancy ingredients. Being a bloke I've simplified it a little, but it still tastes fantastic.

THE KEY: Make sure the bread is well and truly dipped. And let that chilling happen for as long as possible. Otherwise you end up with a white bottom on your chocolate pud.

Suggestion
- *Like the bread pudding, this is lifted to new heights if you use croissants instead of bread.*

Degree of Difficulty: 3   **Serves** 8

Ingredients

1 cup cream

1 cup milk

150 g chopped dark chocolate

3 eggs

⅓ cup sugar

½ teaspoon cinnamon

6 slices thick white bread, each cut in half

½ cup raisins or sultanas (optional)

icing sugar for dusting

Oven temp:
180°C

Method

1. Preheat the oven to 180°C.
2. Combine the cream and milk in a pot over a low heat.
3. When it's warm, add the chocolate chunks and stir until they've melted.
4. Whisk the eggs, sugar and cinnamon together in a bowl.
5. Slowly add the warm chocolate mixture to the egg mixture, whisking as you go, so that you end up with a runny chocolate custard.
6. Dip each piece of bread in the custard and arrange in a baking dish of about 30 cm long and 20 wide so that they overlap (this dessert's gotta have depth). Pour the rest of the custard over the bread to cover (there should be enough to do this).
7. Cover and chill for at least 30 minutes but preferably 1 hour.
8. Bake for about 30 minutes.
9. Once it's baked, dust with icing sugar before serving warm.

CRÊPES

HERE'S WHERE I do you a really big favour. For the next few minutes I am Hutch to your Starsky, I am Goose to your Maverick, I am your wingman.

If you're a bloke in a relationship, and particularly if you're a bloke in a marriage, you'll be familiar with the dog box. This recipe is your ticket out. Mark this page now and let me tell you the exact moment you're going to flick back to it. You're home later than you said you would be, you've been moved to the couch or at least offered the cold shoulder. You wake up Saturday or Sunday morning and . . .

That's when you do it, come back to this page, i.e. make these beautiful thin pancakes and serve them to your beloved with a little lemon juice and sugar or maple syrup.

THE KEY: The secret is in the cooking. Get your skillet or frying pan a little hotter than medium and throw in a small knob of butter. Run that around the base of the pan then pour in about 4 tablespoons of the mixture and start swirling the pan so it works its way out to the edge.

TOP TIP

Okay men, listen up – this is important. Get yourself a good fish slice with a flat bottom edge. Essential for making crêpes. Once you've worked the batter around the pan by swirling the pan itself, use the edge of the fish slice to work it around even further. The point here is to get the crêpe as thin as possible. It sounds like a bit of mucking around, but it's not. And once you get the hang of it you'll be proud of the paper-thin crêpes you're putting out.

Degree of Difficulty: 3

Makes about 8–10 crêpes (if you get them thin enough).

Ingredients

1½ cups standard flour

¼ teaspoon salt

2 eggs

½–¾ cup milk (you may not need it all)

butter

Method

1. Sift the flour and salt into a bowl.
2. Dig out a little well in the middle of the dry ingredients and crack both eggs in.
3. Now pour in a splash of milk – just a splash, mind, and start mixing with a fork. Keep adding milk and stirring until it gets to the right consistency (which is when you can spot little bubbles in the mixture).
4. Heat a little butter in a frying pan. Pour in about ¼ cup of batter (though this will depend a little on the size of the pan). Now swirl it around as I mentioned earlier and let it cook for 1–2 minutes. The crêpe's done on the first side when the mixture is no longer runny on top. Flip it and cook the other side.

Suggestions

- *Try them with chocolate sauce and ice cream.*
- *Whip up some of the super easy Chocolate Mousse (see page 136) and have a crack at this very French dessert:*
  - *Fold warmed crêpe's in half, then in half again to make some triangular cone shapes.*
  - *Spoon some already set mousse into each warm cone.*

NO-BAKE CHOCOLATE TART

A FEW YEARS AGO my wife and I were in Paris's Quartier Latin on our honeymoon. We'd wandered across the Pont des Artes and into a bustling area full of music and restaurants. It's an incredible city, Paris. And the food is amazing. We went to a place down a side street that I'll never find again, no matter how hard I look, into a tiny late-night café that served, among other things, garlic snails.

It's no secret to the rest of the world that snails are not for eating; they are for accidentally standing on in the rain. No matter how much garlic and butter you soak a snail in, it's still a snail. I don't think I have to tell you that in that small but perfectly formed restaurant I did not eat the snails. I had the steak. And followed it with their chocolate tart.

It was delicious. I was inspired. And so, for your baking pleasure, I now present my own take on that luxurious French tart.

 THE KEY: Pressing the base into the tart tin so that it's even across the base and up the sides.

Suggestion

- *If you can get your hands on some white chocolate, shave some of that on top and serve with a scoop of vanilla ice cream. Or, if you want to go all chocolate all the time, use chocolate ice cream instead.*

Degree of Difficulty: 3   **Serves** 8

Ingredients

Base:
125 g butter, melted
1 heaped tablespoon cocoa
1 x 250 g packet wine biscuits

Filling:
250 ml crème fraiche
200 g dark chocolate, finely chopped
30 g butter at room temperature
1 teaspoon bourbon or rum
extra chocolate for decorating

Method

1. Make the base first. Melt the butter and cocoa in a pot over a low heat.
2. Blast the biscuits in a food processor until they're fine crumbs. Pour the crumbs into the pot and mix together thoroughly.
3. Press the biscuit mixture firmly into the bottom of a 20–21 cm tart tin. You may not need all of it.
4. Stick the base in the fridge while you do the rest.
5. To make the filling, warm the crème fraiche in a pot over a medium heat.
6. As soon as it starts to bubble, take it off the heat and chuck in the chopped chocolate and butter.
7. Stir well, then add the bourbon. Keep stirring until smooth.
8. Pour into the base and stick it in the fridge to chill for at least 3 hours.
9. Shave the extra chocolate over the top before serving. The easiest way to get shaved chocolate is to make sure it's room temperature and use a potato peeler or cheese slice. Cold chocolate will chip.

APPLE AND CINNAMON TOASTIE

THERE'S A LESSON in this recipe and it's this: if you keep a thing for long enough it comes back into fashion. AC/DC T-shirts and HQ Holdens, for example. We were fossicking around in the cupboards looking for something else when I dragged out an old toastie-pie maker. These days most of your big city cafés use a press to do panini-style sandwiches and the poor old toastie machine has been left alone like the ugly bridesmaid at your cousin's wedding.

Well, it's back. And unlike your cousin, it's proving to be both useful and popular.

 See if you can find a nice big loaf of raisin or fruit bread. Small slices don't go all the way to the edge of the pie maker.

Suggestions

- *Stew up whatever fruit you like and, if you don't have fruit bread, use white bread. It'll still taste good.*
- *These toasties make a seriously delicious dessert or even Sunday morning breakfast if you treat it like French toast. Extra touches include dusting with icing sugar and serving with a scoop of ice cream; sprinkling with an icing sugar and cinnamon combo and pouring maple syrup over the top; or serving with slices of crisp apple or berries – or both with maple syrup.*

Degree of Difficulty: 1   **Makes** 2

Ingredients

2 apples, cored, peeled and diced

2 dessertspoons sugar

water

4 slices fruit bread

1 teaspoon brown sugar

1 teaspoon cinnamon

Method

1. Preheat the toastie-pie maker.
2. Chuck the diced apple into a pot with the sugar and a splash of water. Cover the pot with the lid and cook it slowly over a low heat to make stewed apple.
3. Butter 2 slices of the fruit bread and place them butter-side down in the hot toastie maker.
4. Spoon some stewed apple onto each slice and sprinkle with a little brown sugar and cinnamon.
5. Top each with a slice of bread, butter-side up, and close the sandwich maker.
6. Cook for about 3–4 minutes.

INDIVIDUAL PEACH PIES

IN MY MID-TWENTIES I lived in a run-down dump of an apartment above a menswear store. There were four of us and the deal with the landlord was that we'd get a break on the rent if we did the place up. So we gibbed and filled and sanded and painted. One of the guys even made a breakfast bar and although it was a lot of hard work we had a blast.

Once the work was done we threw a party and invited a bunch of people we hardly knew. We had a live band. Which is better than a dead band, I guess. One of the songs they did was by a group called 'Presidents of the United States of America'. The song was 'Peaches'.

It's a short song, but they still manage to squeeze in the word 'peaches' 27 times. That's a lot of peaches.

THE KEY: You need the right dishes to pull this off properly. Some good-sized ramekins are best, or metal spring-form moulds that you can lift away if you want to be really impressive.

Degree of Difficulty: 2   **Makes** 4–6

Ingredients

Base:

125g butter

1 x packet wine biscuits

Filling:

250 ml crème pâtissière (see page 168)

1 x 400 g can peaches in juice, drained

Method

1. Make the base first. Melt the butter in a pot over a low heat.
2. Blast the biscuits in a food processor until they're fine crumbs. Pour the crumbs into the pot with the butter and thoroughly mix.
3. Press the biscuit mixture firmly into the bottoms of 4–6 ramekins (depending on the size), then stick them in the fridge to chill while you make the crème pâtissière.
4. Spoon the crème pâtissière on top of each biscuit base and smooth it out with the back of a teaspoon. Then that goes back into the fridge for an hour or so.
5. Dice the peaches and arrange on top of the crème pâtissière.

AUNT UNA'S FRUIT SPONGE
(Gordon McBride)

I SAW GORDON'S BAKING GENIUS first-hand at an inter-company 'bake-off'. The man had made a carrot cake with the most elaborate and impressive display of icing. If this cake had been a bird it would have been a peacock!

This recipe is much more down to earth. Gordon tells me it came from his Aunt Una. According to him, it's true-blue Southland farming cuisine; very basic but a winner every time. It was popular with shearers and especially fortifying after a hard day's lambing, tailing or haymaking. Use a medium-sized baking tin. Of course, if you want to feed a bunch of shearers, I'd suggest quadrupling it and using a very large tin.

THE KEY: Getting it mixed and into the oven pretty smartly after you've added the baking soda. The chemical reaction starts as soon as that soda hits the milk and if you faff around, the sponge won't rise as well.

Note
Use any sort of tinned fruit that takes your fancy. Sliced peaches are good but you can use a combination of, say, a medium tin of sliced peaches and the same of black plums. You could try fresh fruit but this recipe works best with fruit in its own syrup.

Degree of Difficulty: 3   **Serves** 4–6

Ingredients

125 g butter

½ cup sugar

2 eggs

½ teaspoon vanilla essence

1 cup standard flour

1 heaped teaspoon baking powder

¼ cup milk

1 x 350–400 g can sliced or whole fruit

icing sugar for dusting

Oven temp: 180°C

Method

1. Preheat the oven to 180°C.
2. Cream the butter and sugar until light and fluffy.
3. Beat the eggs in, one at a time, beating well after each addition.
4. Stir in the vanilla.
5. Sift the flour and baking powder, then fold into the creamed mixture.
6. Add enough milk to give it a soft 'dropping' consistency.
7. Drain the fruit and arrange it on the bottom of the baking tin, then pour the cake mixture over the top.
8. Bake for about 35 minutes.
9. Dust with icing sugar and serve with vanilla ice cream. Yum.

CHOCOLATE MOUSSE

IN THE CANADIAN REGION of Saskatchewan there's a town called Moose Jaw. The townsfolk swim in the Moose Jaw River and tourists flock to the Tunnels of Moose Jaw, the Moose Jaw Trolley, and the World's Largest Moose.

The Moose Jaw moose stands 32 feet tall, is made of 10 tons of concrete, metal piping and mesh. The ironic tale of the Moose Jaw moose is that a couple of years back the jaw of the Moose Jaw moose actually fell off. I saw it with my own eyes in the Visitors' Centre. I had to ask, 'Is this the Moose Jaw moose jaw?'

That moose is a chocolate sort of colour. But this mousse is not that kind of moose.

 Folding. Normally you fold so it's just combined. This time you fold gently but make sure it's really well mixed.

Suggestion

- *Try Mousse Shooters or Champagne:*
  Pour the just-mixed mousse into wide champagne glasses (not flutes) or into those tall thin shot glasses. Wipe the rims so there's no excess mess and chilled until you're ready to serve them. Decorate with a splash of liquid cream on top.

Note

Once it's chilled you can stir some more whipped cream through. Try plopping it on and then stirring round in a circle to get a marbled effect. Looks nice, tastes great.

Degree of Difficulty: *2*

Serves *6–8* (depending on the size of the glasses)

Ingredients

120 g dark chocolate

30 g butter

2 large eggs, separated

4 tablespoons cream

pinch of salt

½ teaspoon vanilla essence

3 tablespoons sugar

Method

1. Combine the chocolate and butter in a pot and melt over a low heat.
2. Add the egg yolks, 1 at a time, and whisk until smooth.
3. Add the cream and whisk in well.
4. In a separate bowl beat together the egg whites, salt and vanilla (you'll get best results using an electric beater) adding the sugar 1 tablespoon at a time.
5. When the beaten egg whites form stiff peaks, fold them gently but thoroughly into the chocolate mixture.
6. Chill for at least 2 hours.

BOURBON CHOCOLATE TRUFFLES (Brogan Lennane)

I MADE THESE and gave them away as Christmas presents after Brogan first gave me the recipe. The genius of them lies in their simplicity. It's also proof that no idea is better than one that comes from a mate over a quiet beverage.

Brogan told me they started off being experimental. It was in the summer and he was having a few beers with some mates after work, as you do. One of the lads said they marinated their steaks in bourbon before chucking them on the barbie. It just so happened he had been looking for that something special to add to truffles, so being a seasoned baker, he knew straight away the bourbon was worth a try. He whacked it in and from there they were a favourite!

THE KEY: Take your time. Brogan's instructions include opening and enjoying an amber brew as you bake. So, melt and sip and stir and sip and work your way through this recipe in a relaxed fashion.

Suggestion

- *Try rolling the truffles in something other than coconut. I got a good result from using some powdered chocolate that we had left over. Not cocoa, mind. Chocolate.*

Degree of Difficulty: 3   **Makes** 20

Ingredients
50 g butter
100 g chopped chocolate
1 cup icing sugar
2 tablespoons bourbon
1 teaspoon cocoa
desiccated coconut

Method
1. Open a beverage of your choice.
2. Put the butter and chocolate in a pot and heat slowly until both have melted.
3. Add half a cup of icing sugar and stir until just thick.
4. Stir in the bourbon and cocoa and add more icing sugar until the mixture is stiff.
5. Roll into balls, big or small, then roll in the coconut.
6. Chill until ready to serve.
7. Celebrate with another brew.

CREAMY RUM TRUFFLES

TRUTH BE TOLD, despite the name, the kind of booze you use in these doesn't matter. In fact, there's nothing to say that you have to use booze at all. It might be worth trying something like strong coffee instead.

Either way, though, these are for the grown-ups. Where Brogan's Bourbon Truffles are the perfect Antipodean bloke's little bit of rough on the side, these are a late night in Belgium without the wife. They'll make you think of the way silk knickers glisten under a red light and how much you have to spend to see them hit the floor.

THE KEY: Melt the chocolate slowly. A proper chef would use a bain marie, but I find that to be too much palaver for chocolate. Just go gently on the heat and, if you need to, lift the pan away from the element.

Suggestion

- *The cocoa adds a fantastic bitterness to the very rich, creamy truffle, but if you want to make some dark brown and some white, roll some of them in icing sugar.*

Degree of Difficulty: 3   **Makes** 20

Ingredients

   200 g dark chocolate, chopped

   100 g butter, chopped

   100 g icing sugar

   3–4 tablespoons rum (or whisky or bourbon)

   100 ml crème fraiche

   50 g cocoa (for rolling in – not you, the truffles)

Method

1. Melt the chocolate and butter over a very low heat as described earlier.
2. Add the icing sugar bit by bit. Then add the crème fraiche and stir until it's really smooth.
3. Slide in the rum and keep stirring. It'll look really lovely and rich, and not as thick as you think it should be. Don't worry about it – everything is fine.
4. Pour it into a bowl, cover with plastic clingfilm or tin foil and stick it in the fridge for at least 12 hours. That's right – 12 hours!
5. Bring out the bowl, get yourself a spoon and roll the mixture into balls, coating them in the cocoa as you go.

CHOCOLATE CHEESECAKE
(Vicki Coats)

IF YOU GET IN A BOAT at the southern end of Stewart Island the next bit of land you're likely to hit is the icy Antarctic. The most populated area of Stewart Island is a place called Oban. In that part of the world they call visitors 'loopies', the locals are mostly hardened fisher-folk, and when an outsider walks into the local pub the piano player stops and people look at him like he was recently peeled off the bottom of a white gumboot. At least, that's what happened to me when I walked into the pub one frosty evening.

Vicki, however, has no such trouble. She impresses all and sundry with her baking ability. Here is the tale of how she created this chocolate wonder.

She'd been looking online for a dessert to make that didn't need any cooking because sometimes it was just too much hassle to light the coal range and get it to a good baking temperature and keep it that way! After a bit of searching, she combined a few recipes and came up with this. After taking it to a few parties and potluck dinners she got asked for the recipe so often that she wrote it down in a way that the blokes in Oban would understand; drinking instructions included!

THE KEY: Folding. You have to whisk and beat and be aggressive for the first stage and then pull back and fold gently to achieve the lightness and texture a cheesecake needs. It also helps to have a few clean bowls lined up before you start.

Degree of Difficulty: 4   **Serves** 8–10

Ingredients
Base:

50 g butter

80 g crushed biscuits (malt or superwine)

20 g white chocolate chips

Topping:

250 g cream cheese

100 g sugar

2 eggs

150 ml cream

100 g dark chocolate

2 heaped teaspoons powdered gelatine

¼ cup boiling water

Method
1. Make the base first. Line the bottom of a 21 cm spring-form tin with a circle of baking paper. Stick it down with some spray oil or butter.
2. Put the butter in a pot over a medium heat to melt and add the crushed biscuits and chocolate chips. Mix well.
3. Press the mixture into the bottom of the tin and chill for as long as it takes to get the rest sorted out.
4. To make the topping, combine the cream cheese and sugar and beat the crap out of it until smooth.
5. Separate the eggs, then add the yolks to the cream cheese mixture and beat the hell out of it again.
6. In another bowl, whip up the egg whites until they're good and stiff.

[Continued overleaf]

7. In yet another bowl whip up the cream until it's reasonably firm but don't let it turn to butter.

8. Slowly melt the dark chocolate, then mix it in with the cream cheese/sugar mixture.

9. Dissolve the gelatine in the boiling water. Make sure it's completely and 100% dissolved. Add the liquid to the cream cheese/sugar mixture and mix well, then gently fold in the beaten egg whites.

10. Lastly fold in the cream (gently, remember), making sure everything is well combined.

11. Dump the topping on top of the chilled base, smoothing it out so it's evenly distributed and stick back in the fridge for about 2 hours.

Suggestion

- *Once it's suitably chilled decorate the top with grated chocolate and/or chocolate chips. Then serve in decent-sized wedges with some whipped cream and/or berries. So good!*

FILO MORO
(Justin Rae)

JUSTIN AND HIS WIFE – who was then the girlfriend – were at a local restaurant early on in the relationship. They'd been told to ask for the 'Moro dessert', but when they did the waitress didn't know what they were talking about. 'The dessert with a Moro Bar in it,' said Justin. 'Oh,' she said. 'You're not supposed to know it's a Moro. That's the secret ingredient.' Said Justin: 'We hate to break it to you, love. The secret's out.'

Anyway, when it came out it tasted great and he reckoned he'd be able to give it a crack at home. So he did. And it's what sealed the deal with the wife. Great dessert, easy to make, and no secret.

 THE KEY: Keep an eye on the baking process and whip 'em out golden. Serve warm if you can.

Degree of Difficulty: 1

Ingredients

Per person:
1 Moro bar
2 sheets filo pastry

melted butter
1 banana
ice cream

Oven temp: 170°C

Method
1. Preheat the oven to 170°C.
2. Line a baking tray with a sheet of greased baking paper.
3. Wrap each Moro in two layers of pastry.
4. Fold in the ends, then lightly brush with a bit of melted butter.
5. Bake for about 15–18 minutes.
6. Once they're done, serve with the banana and a scoop of ice cream.

LEMON FUDGE CHEESECAKE

WE HAD A BAKING COMPETITION at work which was judged by the head chef at a multi-award winning restaurant. A very good bloke named Sean. Now, without wanting to sound like a big-headed arrogant sort of a nutmeg, I thought I had a pretty good shot in this competition. So instead of doing something obvious like, say, chocolate chip biscuits, I pulled out the big guns. My very own cheesecake creation.

There were a lot of entries for the big bake-off and some of them looked good. I actually got a little nervous. Perhaps my cheesecake wasn't going to be enough!

Sean took a little taste of each entry, offering a comment as he went until he came to my cheesecake. The spoon glided through the cheesy topping, dug into the biscuit bottom and disappeared into his wide-open gob. He said not a thing. As he glanced at me a bead of sweat broke away from my hairline and took off down my forehead. The pressure was mounting.

Turns out he liked it. Not enough to win, though. One of the women baked some chocolate chip biscuits which took the title.

THE KEY: A little plastic clingfilm goes a long way to saving your butt on this one. Line the cake tin as instructed so you can pull out the cheesecake when it's set.

Suggestion

- Before serving the cheesecake, chuck it into the freezer for 20 minutes and then grate lemon zest over the top. Honest to God, it's unbelievable.
- You can also swap the lemon juice for orange or lime. Both work well with the chocolatey base.

Degree of Difficulty: 4   **Makes** 8-ish

Ingredients

Base:
1 x 250 g packet wine biscuits
125 g butter, melted
1 heaped tablespoon cocoa

Topping:
¼ cup lemon juice (no pips)
2 teaspoons powdered gelatine
250 g cream cheese, at room
    temperature
1 cup caster sugar
1 cup evaporated milk, well chilled
1 cup cream

Method

1. Make the topping first. Warm the lemon juice in a small pot and when it gets hot enough (but not boiling) stir in the gelatine to dissolve it. Set the pot to one side.
2. To make the base, melt the butter and cocoa together in a pot over a low heat.
3. Blast the biscuits in a food processor until they're fine crumbs. Pour the crumbs into the pot and mix thoroughly.
4. Line a 20–21 cm cake tin with a large sheet of plastic clingfilm so there's lots of overhang (this will help pull it out afterwards).
5. Press the biscuit mixture into the bottom of the cake tin.
6. To make the topping, combine the cream cheese, caster sugar and the lemon/gelatine mixture into a food processor and blend until smooth.
7. Tip in the chilled evaporated milk and blend a little more.
8. Whip the cream until thick and fold it into the mixture until well combined.
9. Pour the mixture onto the crumb base.
10. Cover and chill in the fridge overnight.

MINI ÉCLAIRS

THEY'RE A FUNNY BUNCH of blokes, the French. They believe Frank Sinatra is French and that the rest of the world is pronouncing his name incorrectly (it should be Fronk). They translate that song 'The Lion Sleeps Tonight' so that it says 'The Lion is Dead This Evening' (go ahead, ask someone French if you don't believe me). And one of their most delectable creations has a very odd name.

The word éclair means lightning in French. And the dough with which you make éclairs is called choux pastry. Choux is the French word for cabbage.

So this is delicious, cream-filled lightning cabbage. Go figure.

THE KEY: Just like those blokes that dive from the high board at the Olympics, it's all about timing your entry. Put the eggs in while everything is still very hot and you'll cook them. So wait until the pastry cools a little first.

Suggestion

- *Top these with chocolate icing or maybe even golden syrup for a sweet alternative. If you're not keen on chocolate, try vanilla icing (see page 160) or just dust them with icing sugar.*

Degree of Difficulty: 3 **Makes** 12

Ingredients

Pastry:

1 cup water

50 g butter, chopped

¼ teaspoon salt

1 cup standard flour

3 eggs

Filling:

250 ml crème pâtissière (see page 168)

Method

1. Preheat the oven to 200°C.
2. Make the pastry first. Combine the water, butter and salt in a pot and bring to a low boil.
3. Get out your power tools, i.e. electric beater – it's essential here. Remove from the heat and add the sifted flour, bit by bit, beating as you go.
4. When you've got a solid ball rolling around in the pot, add the eggs and keep beating until you've got a good, stiff dough.
5. Drop heaped teaspoonsful onto a greased or lined baking tray.
6. Bake for about 10–12 minutes.
7. Once they've cooled, cut a small opening in each ball of pastry and fill it with crème pâtissière.

BLUEBERRY TART

IF YOU ARE A PANTS-WEARING rugby-watching face-shaving bloke and turn up with one of these, it's likely no one will believe you made it. You'll be the victim of ugly gender-based discrimination.

'It can't be,' they'll say.

'Are you sure it wasn't your wife?' they'll say.

'Pass the ice cream,' they'll say.

But the last laugh will be yours when the doubters have to eat humble pie – while everyone else is tucking into this. And the best part of all is that if you have some homemade frozen pastry tucked away, all you have to do is whip up some crème pâtissière and you're most of the way there.

 THE KEY: Making crème pâtissière. Once you've got that nailed you'll be fine. From there it's an assembly job.

Note

You can, of course, use bought sheets of pastry, in which case you'll need about 1½ sheets.

Suggestion

- *Not that you need to be told, but you don't have to use blueberries for this. I've done exactly the same topped with strawberries or a mixture of the two.*

Degree of Difficulty: 4   **Serves** 8

Ingredients

sweet shortcrust pastry (bought or see page 116.
   You'll need about half of that recipe for this.)
250–300 ml crème pâtissière (see page 168)
2 punnets blueberries
icing sugar for dusting

Oven temp:
200°C

Method

1. Preheat the oven to 200°C.
2. Roll out the pastry and press it into the base and up the sides of a greased 20–21 cm pie tin.
3. Bake blind for 15 minutes (see page 114), then remove the baking paper and rice and bake for 1 minute further to brown.
4. Whip it out and let it cool a little.
5. Half to three-quarters fill the pastry crust with crème pâtissière and chuck the blueberries on top.
6. Dust with icing sugar just before you serve it.

PEAR CLAFOUTIS

HERE ARE SOME words and phrases you may find useful if you're ever in France:

- Bisous (kiss)
- Vous êtes très belle (you are very beautiful)
- Combien? (how much?)
- Désolé, je n'ai pas d'argent (sorry, I don't have any money)
- Au revoir, vieux sac (goodbye, old, unattractive woman)
- Another useful word to have in the arsenal is 'clafoutis'. Essentially it means a tart that doesn't need pastry. In other words, it's dead easy.

The second most tempting thing to do now would be to take the phrase 'easy tart' and turn it into some sort of sexist gag. But I won't, because the first most tempting thing is to make and eat the clafoutis. So get on with it.

 THE KEY: Watch the clock. After 15 minutes in the oven turn it down from 200°C to 180.

Note

If you don't have any yoghurt just throw in 1 teaspoon of vanilla essence. Don't sweat the liquid content – there's plenty as it is.

Suggestion

- *The traditional French way of making this involves laying the pear slices on their sides. But I find they fit better lying on their backs. Yes, this too could be turned into a sailor's joke, but we have some baking to do.*

Degree of Difficulty: 3   **Serves** 8

Ingredients

4 pears
4 eggs
100 g standard flour (sifted)
100 g sugar
300 ml cream
2 tablespoons vanilla yoghurt (optional)

Oven temp:
200°C

Method

1. Preheat the oven to 200°C.
2. Grease a 23–26 cm solid-bottomed tart tin (the lift-out kind is no good here because the eggy mixture will pour out the bottom as it bakes).
3. Peel and quarter the pears. Cut each quarter into two slices.
4. Lay the pear slices in the prepared tin.
5. Chuck the remaining ingredients into a bowl and beat with an electric beater until you get a smooth and creamy batter that's starting to thicken just a little.
6. Pour the batter evenly over the pears.
7. Bake for about 15 minutes, then turn down the oven to 180°C and bake for a further 30 minutes.

EASY APPLE TART

IT SHOCKED ME to learn recently that Brad Pitt and Jennifer Aniston are no longer an item. It shocked me even more when I told the wife and she said they'd parted ways a while back. The women's mags I read are in fish and chip shops or doctors' surgeries so the pop culture information I'm privy to can often be out of date. But even if I am ignorant in the ways of Hollywood, I had heard of Paris Hilton; Queen of the Socialites. This is the Paris Hilton of dessert recipes; not too many moving parts, looks quite nice when it's done, and it's easy.

THE KEY: Cut the pastry so there's plenty of overhang. I use the bottom of the tart tin as the guide. Then just fold it back over before baking to give the tart a rustic, crimped look.

Suggestion

- *If you want a tidier result use the traditional method of using the edge of the tart tin to trim the pastry at the top edge. If you do this, prick the pastry with a fork and stick it back in the fridge for another 30 minutes before baking.*

Degree of Difficulty: 2   **Serves** 8

Ingredients

shortcrust pastry (see recipe on page 116. You'll need
        about half of that recipe for this. Freeze the rest.)
3–4 teaspoons apricot jam
3–4 apples (peeled, cored and chopped up)
1 teaspoon cinnamon
6–8 tablespoons sugar

Oven temp:
190°C

Method

1. Preheat the oven to 190°C.
2. Roll out the pastry until it's about 2 mm thick and press it into a 23 cm greased tart tin, making sure there's plenty of overhang – trim so that the overhang is roughly even.
3. Use the back of a teaspoon to rub the apricot jam around the pastry base.
4. Chuck in the chopped apples, packing them in nice and tight. Sprinkle the cinnamon over the apples.
5. Lift up the pastry edge and fold it over on itself. Press it down gently.
6. Sprinkle sugar over the top including the pastry edge.
7. Bake for about 25–30 minutes or until golden brown.
8. After baking, dust with icing sugar and serve warm with ice cream.

1 INGREDIENT ICE CREAM

HERE'S A QUICK POP QUIZ.

- What was it that Alex Foley stuffed into the car exhaust of the two officers tailing him in *Beverly Hills Cop 1*?
- The skin of which fruit is the most commonly used 'slapstick' prop in movie and television gags?
- What's on the cover of The Velvet Underground's debut album?
- What does my wife say I'm driving her most days?
- What one ingredient can be used to make ice cream with no added sugars, sweeteners, colours, flavours, preservatives or fats, and also manages to be fat- and dairy-free?

Here's a clue: the answer to all five questions is the same. Bananas!

My mate Joel reckons that if you feel creative, try adding berries, chocolate, fresh/frozen fruits or anything that you think might taste nice with banana! Super easy, delicious, healthy treat for those hot summer afternoons.

THE KEY: Did you ever read *The Hitchhiker's Guide to the Galaxy*? The key to this is the same as the instruction in that book. Don't panic. You'll think after a couple of minutes that this isn't working. It is.

TOP TIP

Take Joel's advice and add honey, chocolate syrup, maple syrup, peanut butter, flavoured extracts, or additional frozen fruits.

Degree of Difficulty: 1   **Serves** 4–6

Ingredients
3–4 chopped bananas, frozen

Method
1. Add the chunks of frozen banana to the blender bit by bit. At first, the bananas will resist. Don't panic. They'll soon reach that nice chunky stage that you can use in smoothies.
2. But you're not done yet! Keep that blender running for another 3–4 minutes and watch in amazement as what were once frozen bananas turn into a rich, creamy, silky blend.
3. Eat.

REVIEWS

Mat: *This is absolutely bl**dy fantastic!*

Sauces, Icings and *Fillings*

Understanding the Lingo

Ice. (v) pron: AY-ss

a) *To kill.*

b) *Descriptive: commonly used in reference to women who look at (you) with disdain, appear hard-hearted or simply find you unattractive. Eg: she's as cold as ...*

c) *Blocks of frozen water used to cool drinks such as whisky or bourbon. See also, on the rocks.*

This one's easy, right? The thing of it is, though, there are plenty of ways to skin this particular cat. The most common mistakes with icing are: putting it on a cake that's still too hot or making it too runny. Icing should be thick, so you can spread it on evenly. Unless, that is you're deliberately making a thin icing. Sometimes the best way to add a little flavour without going nuts is a sort of sauce over the cake and whatever is served with it.

' *Ice, ice, baby.* **'**

– Vanilla Ice

' *England is a country of 360 religions and three sauces. France has three religions and 360 sauces!* **'**

– With apologies to Voltaire

STANDARD ICING

THE ADVANTAGE, I'm told by friends who know about fashion, of having something black in the wardrobe is that black goes with anything. A black singlet, for example, will go with any of your jeans or shorts and any shade of jandal or work-boot.

The term 'goes with anything' could also be applied to any of the following: Brittany Spears, Paris Hilton and Lindsay Lohan.

It also works for this next icing. Make it good and thick and choose the flavour according to what you're using it for.

Citrus or Vanilla Icing

Degree of Difficulty: 1   **Makes** Enough for 1 cake

2 cups icing sugar
about 2 tablespoons hot water
½ teaspoon vanilla essence or juice of ½ lemon
½ teaspoon butter

1. Chuck everything in a bowl except the butter and stir like crazy.
2. Add the butter and keep stirring.
3. Pour it over the cake – or whatever you're icing – and give it a few minutes to set.

TOP TIP
Hold a knife under hot water for a few seconds and then use the blade to smooth out the icing.

Chocolate Icing

I'M A MILK CHOCOLATE person, as opposed to a dark chocolate person. My mother-in-law is French and thinks that, on the chocolate front at least, I'm an idiot. The point here is that if you want your icing a little darker, just add a shade more cocoa.

Degree of Difficulty: 1   **Makes** Enough for 1 cake

1½ cups icing sugar
1 tablespoon cocoa
hot water
½ teaspoon butter

1. Chuck the icing sugar and cocoa into a bowl and dribble in about 1 tablespoon of warm water.
2. Stir it up. It needs to be really good and thick if it's going on a cake, but if you're going to tip it over a square or slice you can relax it a little. If it's really hard to stir, or not dissolving, gradually add a little more water (notice I said 'gradually').
3. Stir in the butter, which will help give it a nice chocolatey smoothness, like Barry White.

BUTTER ICING

COOL THINGS you can do with butter include:
- When the wife asks you to untangle a necklace rub a little butter into the tangle. It should help, but even if it doesn't she'll never ask you to do this little job again.
- To help your cat stay put when you move house, smear a little butter on one of his paws. It's a lickable treat for the cat to distract him (then go and soak all the scratches he laid on you while you were messing around with the butter).
- If you run out of shaving cream, try using a little butter to smooth the way for your razor (this may also result in the cat wanting to lick your face all day).
- Squeaky doors can be aided by rubbing a little butter into the hinge. These days, it's less expensive to use oil or grease.
- Another great thing to do with butter is make this icing. It's thick and rich compared to standard icing. Of course, it also has a higher fat content. Here are two ways to make butter icing.

Tangy Butter Icing

PAT YOUR POCKETS and check right now. If you don't have any cream cheese on you – and I usually don't – try this one on a carrot cake.

Degree of Difficulty: 1   **Makes** Enough for 1 cake

50 g butter
1 cup icing sugar
juice of ½ lemon or orange

1. Chop the butter into chunks and zap it for 30 seconds in a covered bowl in the microwave.
2. Stir in the icing sugar with a fork. It needs to get really thick and heavy. If necessary, add more icing sugar until it's hard to stir.
3. Add enough juice to bring it back to a spreadable consistency. If there is not enough juice to do this, then add a little water – a tiny bit at a time.

Chocolate Butter Icing

THIS IS THE ICING I use on fudge cake or slices. The butter makes it smooth and rich, and softens the sickly sweetness of standard chocolate icing.

Degree of Difficulty: 1   **Makes** Enough for 1 cake

50g butter
1 cup icing sugar
2 tablespoons cocoa
2 teaspoons hot water

1. Chop the butter into chunks and zap it for 30 seconds in the microwave.
2. Stir in the icing sugar and cocoa with a fork. You need this to get really thick and heavy. If the 1 cup doesn't do it add more until it's hard to stir.
3. Add a tiny bit of hot water and keep on stirring. Add more if you need to – but carefully.

Note

You can turn either of these two butter icings into vanilla icing just by leaving out either the citrus or chocolate and adding half a teaspoon of vanilla essence along with a little water.

CREAM CHEESE ICING

THERE'S A WOMAN I KNOW who likes to knit jumpers for baby trees and culture her own yoghurt from recycled chickpea husks. Her diet, she told me one exciting afternoon, consists mostly of carrots and cream cheese. 'What a coincidence', I replied. 'I eat a fair bit of both, myself.' I didn't mention the carrots were grated in a cake and the cream cheese was this icing.

Degree of Difficulty: 1   **Makes** Enough for 1 cake

2 tablespoons softened butter
¼ cup cream cheese
1 cup icing sugar
finely grated rind of ½ lemon

1. Beat together the butter and cream cheese until it's nice and smooth and creamy.
2. Slowly mix in the icing sugar and thrash it until it's really well combined. Throw in the grated lemon rind and give it another couple of stirs.

REVIEWS

Luke: *Alison used this on her carrot cake and it was divine!*
James: *This is awesome stuff!*
Haidee: *OMG. Finally!*
Joe: *Wonderful, really delicious.*
Phil: *I leave out the lemon rind and add a splash of vanilla essence.*

ROYAL ICING

SO THERE we were trying to figure out why this is called Royal, when Jonesy came out with this gem. 'It's a puffed-up egg, like most of the Royal family'. And there you have it.

Degree of Difficulty: 1   **Makes** Enough for 1 cake

1 egg white
1 cup icing sugar
food colouring

1. Using an electric beater, beat the egg white with about one-third of the icing sugar.
2. As soon as it starts to puff up, pour in another third of the icing sugar.
3. Beat a little longer and tip in the remaining icing sugar. Keep beating until pulling the beaters out leaves the white peaks pretty much standing on their own.

Note

If you want to make icing in two or three different colours, separate the icing into even amounts and chill for a while. Then, when you're ready to ice your cookies or whatever, add the food colouring as required and mix through.

CUSTARD

CUSTARD OFTEN GETS A BAD RAP, e.g.

> *There once was a girl from Manila*
> *Who had to have custard vanilla*
> *She ate it thrice daily*
> *Would dance around gaily*
> *Singing 'I've got six more jugs in the chiller'.*

Although, to be fair, that's not a rap so much as a limerick. However, when someone uses the phrase 'It's all about to turn to custard', it seems harsh on poor custard because it means that things are about to go bad. But custard is good. So why would people use the word custard in this way? Why not, for example, say something like, 'It's all about to turn to Brussels Sprouts'? That would make much more sense.

 THE KEY: If you don't want scrambled eggs in your custard, add the hot milk nice and slowly.

TOP TIPS

The best way to keep custard warm is to pour it into a ceramic jug and cover the top with plastic clingfilm. Place the jug in another container that's filled with just-boiled or very hot water.

To make caramel custard, add 1 tablespoon of golden syrup to the mixture along with the vanilla.

Degree of Difficulty 1   **Makes** 600 mls

Ingredients

4 egg yolks
2 tablespoons sugar
1 tablespoon flour or cornflour
400 ml milk
200 ml cream
½ teaspoon vanilla essence

Method

1. Combine the yolks in a bowl with the sugar and flour and whisk until smooth.
2. Pour the milk and cream into a pot and bring to the boil over a low to medium heat.
3. Slowly pour the hot milk into the egg mixture, stirring with a whisk.
4. Once it's all mixed in, add the vanilla.
5. Pour the mixture back into the pot over a medium heat and stir until it thickens.

Suggestion

- *There is just no better way to have custard than over diced or chopped peaches. Preferably those that have been preserved lovingly by your mum or grandmother, but a good old tin of peaches in juice will do just as well.*
- *It's also great with Aunt Una's Fruit Sponge (see page 136).*

CRÈME PÂTISSIÈRE

AS GIRLY, FANCY OR FOREIGN as it might sound, crème pâtissière is one of those absolute musts in life. It's not hard to make, it lasts for ages in the fridge and it has a dozen different uses (think sweet tart, profiteroles, éclairs and so on – they all have the stuff in them).

 THE KEY: Easy does it when adding the hot milk. The idea is to slowly warm the rest of the mixture without cooking the egg.

TOP TIP

If you want the final product good and thick use all the flour. But if you prefer it more custard-like, only use two thirds of it.

Once you've poured the crème into a bowl, grease some baking paper with butter and place it on top of the mix. This will stop it forming a skin on top.

Degree of Difficulty: 1   **Makes** 500 mls

Ingredients
3 eggs, separated
100 g sugar
50 g flour
pinch of salt
500 ml milk
½ teaspoon vanilla essence (or a whole vanilla pod is even better)

Method
1. Reserve one egg white and chuck out the other two (unless you fancy collecting a couple more and making a pav).
2. Put all 3 yolks in a bowl with the sugar and whisk until your forearms ache (in other words, until it's nice and frothy).
3. Add the flour, a third at a time, whisking it through every time.
4. Keep whisking, then add the egg white and whisk some more.
5. Pour the milk into a pot, add the vanilla, then bring it to the boil.
6. Slowly pour the milk into the egg mixture, stirring with a spoon or spatula.
7. Once it's all mixed in, transfer it to a clean pot and stick it over a medium heat.
8. Stir until it thickens. It takes a few minutes and then – all of a sudden – it happens.
9. Leave to cool and then chuck it in the fridge to chill.

CHEESE SAUCE

KNOWING HOW TO BEAT UP a good cheese sauce is a 'must know' for any bloke. It's great over broccoli or cauliflower or corned silverside.

Degree of Difficulty: 1   **Makes** 600 mls

Ingredients

pinch of ground pepper
2 tablespoons butter
2 tablespoons standard flour
1 cup milk
½ cup grated tasty cheese

Method

1. Put a pot over a low heat and throw in your pinch of pepper.
2. Once you can smell the pepper, throw in the butter. Keep heat low.
3. As soon as the butter has melted, add the flour bit by bit, stirring.
4. Keep stirring. It'll go quite gluggy and lumpy but stir on, relentlessly.
5. Add the milk slowly, still stirring all the while.
6. Add about half the cheese.
7. After a few minutes, the milk will really start to thicken. At that point add the rest of the cheese and stir until it's melted.

Note

To make a white sauce for something like a fish pie just follow the instructions above, but leave out the cheese.

INDEX

ACKNOWLEDGEMENTS

THERE ARE PLENTY OF PEOPLE to thank for getting this book to the shelf and into your butter-greased fingers, but any self-respecting Bloke should start with his Mum. And in my case, I get to thank my Step-Mum too. Thanks for the recipes, both of you.

Thanks also to Mark Killip at Champion Flour. Without his help and continued support, the website would never have been born. Blokes who bake are Champion Blokes. While we're on those who've supported, thanks to the good people at Bin Inn, particularly Nicolette and Brett.

There are several recipes herein that have been contributed by baking Blokes and Blokettes around the country so thanks to: Jeff Cameron, Joel Edwards, Brendan Tourelle, Brogan Lenane, Ian Cameron, Justin Rae, Gordon McBride, Vicki Coats, Andy Ronaldson, Trevor Carter and Nigel Bradly. I would also like to thank all those who've sent recipes in to the website, blokeswhobake.co.nz.

The great folks at TVNZ's *Good Morning* have also had plenty to do with the success of the website to date. Thanks to everyone who helps make it appear as though I know what I'm doing.

A special thanks to Christine Thomson and her team at New Holland for asking me to have a crack at this and for not telling me how much work it would be.

There are a few people at the Breeze in Wellington who have been especially encouraging throughout and they deserve thanks too. Stu Smith, Kath Bier, Hannah Parkes, Paige Wright and in particular, my understanding bosses.

Thanks also to my wife, Juliette. Not least for taste-testing everything I make. Not all of it is good.

Finally, thanks to two of the best Blokes I've known: Tom Joll and Dave Joll, my father and brother. Because it would have pleased them both immensely to know that they had the last word in this book.

NOTES